Vigilante Killer Grace Fortescue

Sarah Thompson

Published by Trellis Publishing, 2021.

While every precaution has been taken in the preparation of this book, the publisher assumes no responsibility for errors or omissions, or for damages resulting from the use of the information contained herein.

VIGILANTE KILLER GRACE FORTESCUE

First edition. July 8, 2021.

Copyright © 2021 Sarah Thompson.

ISBN: 979-8224715060

Written by Sarah Thompson.

VIGILANTE KILLER

GRACE FORTESCUE
SARAH THOMERSON

Twenty-four years before Emmitt Till, the name Joseph Kahahawai would make its mark as a historical moment of prejudice and racial discrimination that would change the islands of Hawaii forever.

At the end of the 1920s, the stock market had crashed and poverty was sweeping its way across the nation. While those without money and influence suffered, America continued to grow in other ways. Architecture, science, and the arts boomed, even while most Americans were living underneath the intense and crushing pressure of the Great Depression - and would continue to do so for the next ten years.

In the 1930s, the economy in Hawaii was no better than what you would find on the mainland. The history of Hawaii is long and tumultuous, beginning with Polynesian settlers, five hundred long years before British explorers would ever set foot on any of the islands of Hawaii. It wasn't until 1778, after the Kingdom of Hawaii was established with the help of James Cook and the European military, did Americans start to immigrate to the islands. But this brought diseases that the native Hawaiians had never experienced and the population dwindled as a result. Americans would rewrite the constitution of the Kingdom of Hawaii and force them to join the United States as the Territory of Hawaii in 1898.

It's important to understand the tumultuous relationship between the native Hawaiians and the white Americans before one can truly understand the tragic and shocking events that took place in Hawaii in January of 1932. The events of Hawaii's journey from kingdom to territory were not far in the past for many Hawaiians alive at that time - some remembered it well, while others would know the history from their parents who lived through the rise and fall of their own disenfranchisement. By the 1930s, Hawaii was teeming with military personnel from the United States. The U.S Navy was a constant and familiar presence to the islands, particularly Honolulu.

While on the mainland, African Americans were struggling against discrimination in many of the same ways that native Hawaiians were.

Except, the rest of the United States was deeply unaware of the racial injustices that were happening on one of their territories. What most people knew of Hawaii back then consisted of beautiful, sandy beaches and the 'beach boys' that would tend to the people who spent their days sunbathing, surfing, and playing in the water. Hidden beneath this beautiful, tropical facade were slums, ghettos, and poverty-stricken people struggling to make due.

Grace Fortescue, born Grace Hubbard Bell, would not make her way to Hawaii until after her marriage to Granville "Rolly" Fortescue, a U.S Army Major. Fortescue was born on the 3rd of November in 1883, to Charles John Bell, who was the first cousin to the famous Alexander Bell. Fortescue's mother, Roberta, was the daughter of the president of the Bell Telephone Company, Gardiner Hubbard.

After Grace Fortescue was born, her mother would become pregnant again but die during childbirth. After her death, Fortescue's father would go on her marry her aunt, Grace Hubbard. Together, they lived in Washington D.C in their Cleveland Park neighborhood. Fortescue grew up fairly wealthy, though those that knew her as a youth could attest to Fortescue's more playful personality. In her youth, Fortescue made the newspaper twice due to her outrageous ideas for pranks. Once, Fortescue and her friends joined hands on their roller skates and blocked traffic going down Pennsylvania Avenue. Another time, Fortescue and her gang of pranksters stole a trolley for a joy ride.

Grace left her wild ways behind her when she met and married Granville Fortescue. While Grace Fortescue was due a fortune of inheritance when her parents passed, her husband was the first cousin of Theodore Roosevelt. It seemed like a match that would bring financial success to the relationship. However, Fortescue's hopes of living a lavish life would not be coming to fruition but Grace would give birth to three daughters nonetheless. She named them Marion, Thalia, and Kenyon - the last of which would go on to become known as the actress Helene Whitney.

Of all of Fortescue's daughters, it was Thalia that would leave a black mark on the island of Hawaii, dragging her mother along with her. After Thalia married Navy lieutenant Thomas Massie, her husband was stationed in Pearl Harbor. Though it wasn't unheard of, Thalia married Thomas at the young, impressionable age of 16. This brought Thalia Massie, as well as Grace Fortescue, to the island of Honolulu in Hawaii. Mother and daughter did not live far from one another, Thalia Massie living with her husband on Kahawai Street in Manoa Valley, and Fortescue living on Kolowalu Street. It's easy to assume that if Grace Fortescue followed her daughter from Washington D.C to Hawaii, and lived within easy traveling distance, the two were quite close.

What happened the night of September 12th, 1931 would become a point of contention between the native Hawaiians and white American families that were stationed in Pearl Harbor.

That night, Thalia Massie was reluctant to travel with her husband, Thomas, to a hotel called Ala Wai Inn in Honolulu. She would have been going there with her husband and his military friends. Despite not wanting to go, Thomas wouldn't take no for an answer. And so, already in a bad mood, Thalia Massie went with her husband to the hotel and set in motion events that would have a rippling effect through all of Hawaii then would resonate for decades after.

While her husband enjoyed a rancorous good time with his fellow Navy officers and recruits, Thalia remained upstairs. She didn't join them for drinks or Navy talk. By now, Thalia was 20 years old and had spent the last four years of her life as a Navy wife. There's no telling what Thalia was thinking that night as she sat upstairs, waiting for her husband to be done drinking with his friends. Getting married at such a young age puts pressure on any woman, and Thalia had been moved so far from her home and had only her mother there on Honolulu to turn to for familial comfort.

Whatever her thoughts, Thalia Massie decided to leave the Ala Wai Inn by herself. She disappeared into the night - in September, Honolulu would have warm days and nights, with little rain. Thalia, perhaps, saw no harm in slipping out of the Inn into the warm, Honolulu night and hoping to make her way home. Of course, the next time that anyone saw Thalia Massie, it wouldn't be home, safe behind the locked door of her shared apartment with her husband. In fact, Thalia Massie would emerge to the world again just an hour later, stumbling her way along the road, looking harried and pitiable.

A man by the name of Eustace Bellinger found Thalia that night. He was driving along Ala Moana Road, 1 A.M that Sunday morning. He spotted Thalia Massie, and like any concerned samaritan, slowed down to help her. As he slowed down to observe her, it was clear that Thalia Massie was a mess. She was clearly beaten and had an injury to her jaw that would later be found to be broken. Thalia, possibly grateful to see a kind face after whatever ordeal she had just gone through, told Bellinger that she has been beaten by what she called "Hawaiians".

Bellinger helped Thalia back to her home, where she waited for her husband. However, by the time Thomas Massie returned home, Thalia's story had begun to change. Was it the trauma of the event, or was Thalia simply adding more details to punish her husband for making her join him when she didn't want to? When Thomas Massie returned home, Thalia repeated her story of having been jumped and beaten by the Hawaiian men. But now, Thalia added another detail: they had raped her, too.

Repeatedly.

While her husband pressed for details, Thalia couldn't give him much more than that. It was too dark, she said, for her to make out any discerning details. She told him that she hadn't been able to get the license plate of the car they put her in to dump her back on Ala Moana Road. Her husband took her to the hospital, where Thalia was given an exam and the police were called. She gave the same story, now solidifying her version of events from that night. She was walking home, a group of Hawaiian men surrounded her, and she was beaten and raped.

Unfortunately, the evidence gathered at the exam in the hospital didn't support all of Thalia's story. She was clearly beaten and assaulted - that much was visible from her bruises and her broken jaw. But the rape? It didn't seem to the staff that Thalia Massie had suffered a sexual assault. But, that didn't seem to matter to the police. It didn't take long for the police to round up five men, though not all of them were native Hawaiian. Two of them were, while the others were a mix of Chinese and Japanese.

The five men were, to the police, the most likely candidates for such a crime. After all, they were a carload of men driving about that night, and two of them even had criminal records. The men were Henry Chang, Benny Ahakuelo, David Takai, Horace Ida, and Joseph Kahahawai. That same night, the men had gotten into a road rage incident with a local Hawaiian woman by the name of Agnes Peeples, and Kahahawai even admitted to having punched her in a fit of rage. All five were arrested and when presented to Thalia, she began to remember their faces. Or was it all suggestion?

The problem was, all five, including Joseph Kahahawai, were far away from the scene of Thalia's attack. The road rage incident on Agnes Peeples put them far enough away that the investigators were having trouble seeing how it could be humanly possible for the men to have had that altercation, and then driven to where Thalia was in the time allotted for the attack to take place. It was only an hour that Thalia Massie had been missing in the humid, Honolulu night. There wasn't any way to make it work. That didn't seem to matter to the police, or to Thalia. She had clearly been assaulted, but now the question was by who, and why?

The five men, including Joseph Kahahawai, were then arrested and put on trial for the rape and beating of Thalia Massie. Of course, the jury couldn't come to a verdict. Not only was there an issue of the racial divide among the jury, but there was also no hard evidence of the five men having been involved in the assault. The court's inability to prove beyond a reasonable doubt that the five men were involved caused a mistrial, and the men were released on bail to wait for another trial.

Grace Fortescue, who had been by her daughter's side the entire trial, wasn't pleased to hear about the men being released back into the world. After all, her daughter had named them all (or, had she just been shown their faces?) and accused them of assaulting her. It didn't matter that the jury couldn't come to a conclusion as to whether the men did it or not. It also didn't seem to matter that her daughter had changed her story between being found on the side of the road, and the hospital. All that mattered was that something had clearly happened to Thalia Massie, and Grace Fortescue was as protective of her daughter as any mother would be.

Not only was Fortescue furious, but so were the other personnel who were stationed at Pearl Harbor. To Fortescue, and Thalia's husband Lieutenant Massie, the five men were guilty and nothing was going to convince them otherwise. In fact, when the men were released on bail to await a retrial, this only strengthened their conviction even more. What is a mother to do when faced with the release of the men that her daughter accused of assault and rape? What Fortescue and Lieutenant Massie decided to do was along the lines of vigilante justice. Their anger was validated by Yate's Stirling, an admiral who was in charge of Pearl Harbor at the time. Stirling, when hearing of the news, simply said, "Our first inclination is the seize the brutes and string their asses up."

They began with Horace Ida, the driver. A group of white U.S Navy personnel kidnapped Ida and beat him, kicking and punching him. They even threatened to throw him over a cliff that was not far from the site of his beating. Despite it all, Ida managed to escape his attackers and live to see another day. The next target of the team of vigilantes, lead by Grace Fortescue, was Joseph Kahahawai.

In January, several months after Thalia Massie's assault, Grace Fortescue lead a coup to abduct Kahahawai right as he was leaving the courthouse in Honolulu. The abduction was bold, perhaps because they knew that there wouldn't be any consequences for white, U.S Navy personnel taking a Hawaiian man accused of assault off the street. In broad daylight, Fortescue and Lieutenant Massie handed Kahahawai a fake "summons", and then promptly began to shove him into Fortescue's car and take off with him in the back seat.

With Fortescue leading the charge, Lieutenant Massie was joined by two men by the names of Albert Jones and Edward Lord in the abduction of Kahahawai. They returned to Massie's home, where they used torture methods in order to interrogate him. The idea was to force a confession out of Kahahawai. But since there was nothing for him to confess, Kahahawai wouldn't give in. At one point, Kahahawai attempted to escape by lunging at one of his captors. As Kahahawai threw himself at Massie in order to escape, he was shot by Lord and there he died, in Massie's home.

With a dead man on their hands, now, the four vigilantes attempt to remove the body. They wrapped Kahahawai's body in a blanket and move him back to Fortescue's car. Fortescue took the wheel, and at some point during their attempt at escaping unseen to dump the body, a police chase ensued that caused them to be stopped. When the police looked into the car, they found Kahahwai's body, bloody, beaten, bound and finally shot. Strangely enough, the four people still alive in the car had nothing to say for themselves. They didn't deny what they had done, believing their actions to be out of justice for what had been done to Thalia Massie.

And this is where the crime becomes murky. Because, indeed, something had been done to Thalia Massie. A beating, definitely. Rape, perhaps not. But someone had taken advantage of a young woman walking home, alone at night, and done her some great harm. The motivation of Fortescue's orchestration of the abduction, torture, and murder could easily be attributed to Fortescue's very real belief in her daughter's story. And yet, one has to wonder: would they have taken the law into their own hands had the accused men been part of their own world? Could Thalia Massie's accusation of her assault being done by Hawaiian men be a ploy to throw the suspicion off another U.S Navy member? Or even her own husband?

Stirling gave his sympathies to Grace Fortescue, attributing her actions as those of a "brave mother". Newspaper editorials had their own say about the crimes committed - not against Kahahawai, but against Thalia Massie. Some even went so far as to declare Hawaii unsafe for "decent white women". In the 1930s, crimes against women often went unpunished, so it isn't hard to imagine that the outrage was due to the color of Thalia's skin, rather than the crime committed against her as a woman. The public opinion was now sympathetic to Kahahwai's killers, Grace Fortescue especially.

A trial was convened for Lieutenant Massie, Albert Jones, Edward Lord, and Grace Fortescue. At first, the vigilante's are charged with first-degree murder. But after some deliberation, the charges were dropped to second-degree, a charge that would carry a weight much like manslaughter. The idea, of course, being that the four of them were attempting to elicit a confession out of Kahahawai, and his death was accidental.

Well known American attorney, Clarence Darrow, was obtained to defend Massie, Jones, Lord, and Fortescue during the trial. The trial was particularly long, and Darrow originally argued for temporary insanity from Lieutenant Massie's case. Temporary insanity, in terms of the law and defense, is defined when someone loses their sanity during a crime, but later regains it, afterward. The defense is usually used in "crimes of passion", allowing for a lighter sentence or even an acquittal of the crimes entirely if the defense can argue that the defendant wasn't in control of his or her actions at the time that the crime was committed.

Despite Darrow's infamous caseload under his belt and his speech to the jury that begged for their sympathy, he lost the case. Grace Fortescue, along wither her daughter's husband and their two accomplices, were sentenced to ten years of "hard labor" for their crimes. And perhaps, in any other case of vigilante justice that resulted in the torture and death of an innocent man, that would have been that. But the story wasn't over for Grace Fortescue. However, the U.S Navy was a force to be reckoned with, and the Navy wasn't pleased that four of their own were being sentenced to pay for their crimes. After all, many Navy personnel and many white Americans that lived in Honolulu believed that Fortescue and her accomplices had done the right thing in killing Kahahawai.

Governor Lawrence Judd couldn't ignore the pressure from the Navy or the outrage of the public. Instead of allowing the four vigilantes to serve their time was the jury decided, he commuted the sentence to a single hour, which Fortescue and company served in his office. And so, Grace Fortescue, Lieutenant Massie, and their two accomplices essentially got away with murder.

The facts surrounding what would become to be known as the Massie Affair are murky, frustrating, and hard to separate from the context of the time that they occurred in. Joseph Kahahawai was, admittedly, a violent man who had no issue assaulting a woman (Peeples) over a road rage incident. The other men who had been accused had criminal records under their belt. These were not perfect, innocent victims by any means. The racial divide between the native Hawaiians and the white U.S Navy families is also inseparable from the details of the Massie Affair. It's easy to assume that Grace Fortescue and her daughter were scheming white women who wanted to punish non-white men by accusing them of assault and rape.

After all, there's precedence for that exact behavior, especially in a world that was not yet evolved on matters of race and the personhood of those without white skin. Before Grace Fortescue, and even before

Emmett Till, in Alabama, the Scottsboro Boys case exposed an underbelly to the justice system when it came to people of color, white juries, and white accusers. America's past is not a proud one, not all the time, and to see the truth of a situation clearly, it's important to understand that the world had once been like.

However, one could just as easily see Fortescue's frenzied actions as a mother desperate to punish the person her daughter had accused of assault and rape. Could anyone fault a mother for going to any length she could to protect her daughter? And yet, there's no room to deny that race did, indeed, play a role. Whether it was Thalia Massie casting accusations on Kahahawai to divert away from another attacker, or Kahahwai's killers going unpunished because they were white and part of the respected U.S Navy.

So what became of the Massies and Grace Fortescue after the trial, the one hour sentence, and the end of a life that would never face a jury of his peers, as was his right? Well, Lieutenant Massie and Thalia decided to avoid another rape trial for the other four suspects that Thalia had accused. Instead of staying on Honolulu, Thalia and her husband hoped about Malolo, a luxury cruise liner at the time, and found their way to San Francisco. Perhaps the stress of the entire ordeal caused a crack in their marriage, or perhaps there was some other life stressor. Whatever the reason, the Massie marriage ended in divorce.

The other four men were cleared of all charges. After an investigation conducted by a detective agency, there was no substantial evidence that they had committed the assault on Thalia Massie - perhaps because the road rage assault that they did commit gave them an ample alibi. After going through the medical records, they also found no physical evidence that Thalia had been gang-raped by five men.

As for Grace Fortescue, she continued to live out the rest of her aging, greying years in Florida. She died in 1979, at the age of 96 in Palm Beach, Florida. She was able to live a life far past the tender age of

26, the age at which she and her son-in-law and accomplices cut Joseph Kahahawai's life short.

The island of Hawaii, as those that lived there have said, was forever changed by the year-long Massie Affair. It was a point in history that highlighted the way that the people of color, Hawaiian, Japanese, Chinese, Indian or otherwise, were being treated in Hawaii. Before the Massie Affair, and even after, the 1930s were a period where the native Hawaiians were routinely referred to, even in publications, as "half breeds" and "mongrels".

The Massie Affair and Grace Fortescue's role in the whole ordeal became a moment in time that would be a turning point in how native Hawaiians and white Americans would understand the racist system in place that allowed for this crime to take place. At any point, someone might have been able to stop it: the U.S Navy, the court systems, the jury, the Governor, the newspapers, the magazine publications. But each point conspired together, and they all allowed Grace Fortescue to walk free from murder.

HUSBAND KILLER SHARI TOBYNE

ANA BENSON

When it comes to female killers, the most common type of crime is mariticide or murdering their husbands. There are many motivations behind taking someone's life but killing a person so close to you is often fueled by passion, financial gain, jealousy, or betrayal. The case of Shari Tobyne is the perfect example of a woman scorned. Her husband of thirty-five years wanted to divorce her due to the financial problems she caused by mishandling the couple's finances.

So one day before he was set to leave their rented house and move on, Shari snapped. She simply couldn't allow him to leave after so many years they spend together. Shari continued to live her life normally, but Arizona police started uncovering body parts from counties surrounding the city of Phoenix and they couldn't determine the exact identity of the deceased man. Worried Tobyne children alerted the law enforcement that their father was missing and this is where the story started to unravel.

It will soon be discovered that a loving mother and a grandmother murdered her husband in cold blood because leaving him was simply not an option.

Early life

Shari Tobyne was born on 24th of July, 1956 in Clifton, Kansas. She grew up in a rural area just outside of the city. Her parents owned a farm and her father was quite successful in his line of business. She was a happy, carefree girl who enjoyed spending time in nature and would often help her family by jumping in and completing difficult farm related tasks.

This is where she met her future husband, Dwight Tobyne. He lived just across the street from Shari and his parents ran their own agricultural business. Dwight loved Shari's personality and energy so he soon realized that he had a crush on her. However, he didn't want to make a move too quickly so he waited until he got a college acceptance letter to ask Shari to be his girlfriend. She was still in high school at that time.

Both Shari and Dwight wanted to achieve business success and escape their small town. They soon realized that they were a match made in heaven because they cheered each other on and offered great support when needed. The couple married in 1975 and they made a decision to move to Salina, Kansas to start their life as a husband and wife. They wanted to make a better future for their family and relocating to a big city was their best option.

Shari was a bit apprehensive at first but the fact that she had Dwight right there beside her made the transition a lot easier. Dwight started a semester at the University of Kansas, studying Animal Sciences while Shari wanted to be a perfect wife and keep their home in pristine conditions. The pressure was on Dwight and he simply had to succeed with his academic work because he was supposed to carry the Tobyne family to the business success eventually.

The couple's first child, Jennifer was born in 1977. They welcomed a baby boy, Brad only three years later. The family was growing but Dwight was still in college, trying to graduate. Shari was very stressed about the financial situation and they struggled to take care of their children. Dwight did his best to earn some extra money so he landed a part-time job in hopes it would cover the expenses.

Trading stocks and interests were all the rage back in the 1980s and Dwight though it would be a perfect opportunity to invest the money he had on his account and try his luck. It wasn't his field of study and he soon got lost in all the numbers and investment opportunities. He pretty much gambled away all of their family savings and they ended up getting evicted from their townhouse. They packed their things and moved back to their parents.

With a third child on its way, the Tobyne family was under a lot of stress. Dwight even though about leaving Shari because he felt like he had failed both her and their children. Being the provider was already very hard for him and the fact that he managed to spend all of their money created additional pressure. Moving back to their parents was another blow. The situation was dismal and both of them knew that they have to make some difficult decisions in near future.

The move and success

The Tobyne family wanted to have a new beginning so they packed their things and moved to Denver, Colorado. Dwight was ecstatic because he can continue his education up there and earn a master's degree that will certainly come in handy when it comes to finding employment in near future. He also landed a full-time job at a bank and the pay was quite good.

Inspired by the economic boom of the 1990s, Dwight Tobyne enrolled into a business school and earned a diploma after a couple of years. Combining everything he learned with smart ideas and investments, Dwight created a leasing company. It was exactly what Denver needed at the time and he knew it would be a success.

It took Dwight a few years to make some serious money and now the family was living comfortably in a large house. They had everything imaginable and Shari finally started to feel confident. She knew that Dwight was a hard worker but she did have doubts when the company was first started because she knew how it felt to lose money.

The Tobynes looked like a perfect family because they were wealthy, active in the community, and their children were successful in school. Shari loved the attention and enjoyed a classy lifestyle that was a complete opposite of the things they went through in Kansas. She felt the need to contribute to the wealth of her family so she got her real estate license. It was time to stop being a housewife and start doing things on her own.

Dwight supported his wife's decision to create her own business and they cheered each other on as usual. They would often collaborate and help each other out with work-related tasks. Everything seemed to go really well for the Tobynes and they continued to live large with their ever-growing wealth.

The first sign of trouble

In 2003, Shari and Dwight lived alone in their family house. The children have moved out and the two of them still ran their business successfully. One day, Shari told Dwight that she made some mistakes regarding one of her accounts and that the numbers were not adding up. Her client lost their money due to this mistake and Shari's real estate license was taken away. Her job and the real estate career were in jeopardy.

It was clear that Shari tried to commit some type of fraud but she was never prosecuted for that. The Tobynes had plenty of money left in the bank and since they were experts at the new beginnings, they thought it would be the perfect time to move somewhere warmer. Dwight told his friends that they were going to Arizona because the real estate opportunities down there are amazing. But the truth was they were fleeing the city because the majority of their neighbors were aware of Shari's bad business decisions and they needed to surround themselves with people who don't know them well.

They bought a huge house in Gilbert, Arizona which was as posh and classy as their previous residence. It was a part of a gated community outside of Phoenix and they felt right at home. Dwight continued with his leasing business and it seemed like Phoenix was really a good relocation choice because he was getting a lot of work there. Since Shari was not employed, she became very involved with the way Dwight ran his business. She started helping him out because she had plenty of free time on her hands. Shari was in charge of family finances.

But in 2008, Dwight started getting phone calls from his friends and clients who were asking about his health. The majority of them though that he was in a hospital. Dwight figured out that Shari was behind this and that she was telling them that he had a heart-attack. He got really worried and started going through his company's financial records. He noticed something alarming – he was missing a large amount of money and since Shari was in charge of the accounts, he asked her about it.

The confrontation was quite explosive, mostly because Dwight couldn't believe that she could do something like that to him. After all, they have been married for decades and stealing from his own company was simply shocking. Shari had an explanation for everything and she told Dwight that she took the money to pay the bills and other necessities. Dwight was still unconvinced and furious. He knew what she had done in Denver and this looked almost the same.

Just a couple of weeks after the fight, Shari contacted her children and she sounded distracted. They weren't sure what was happening but it was clear that something was very wrong. Dwight was at the house when he realized that he hadn't seen his wife for hours. After combing every room of their home, he went out to his neighbor's house and he found Shari laying on a couch. There was an empty pill bottle right beside her. Shari wasn't responding and he called an ambulance.

Once she was conscious, Shari explained that she did try to kill herself because she simply couldn't take it any longer. She hid important information from Dwight and he found everything out in the hospital. They were in serious debt and their accounts were pretty much emptied out. The reality came crashing down on Dwight and he couldn't hide the sadness from his face. His business was ruined and he worked hard for nothing. He was still in disbelief that his own wife could have done this.

The Tobynes had to sell their lavish house in the gated community in order to cover at least a portion of the debt. It was a psychological shock to both of them because they had to find a smaller place to live in. They were back at the square one. So they gathered their things and moved to Scottsdale, Arizona.

The tensions between the pair were high and Dwight was on the fence about divorcing Shari. He made a decision to leave her in autumn of 2009 because he couldn't forget the things she put him through.

However, they did their best to appear as normal as possible in front of their children. But when Dwight failed to show up at the Thanksgiving dinner in November of 2009, Shari confessed that Dwight left her and moved to Mexico. None of their children could have predicted that Shari was not telling the truth about the divorce and that the reality was more sinister.

The murder of Dwight Tobyne

In November of 2009, Shari bought herself a gun. She started practicing shooting at a local gun range and her last visit to that place was on 22nd of November. It looked like the divorce was the final straw that made her think about murdering her own husband. After getting a sense of how the gun worked, all she needed to do is find the right time to shoot Dwight. The exact date of the murder is still unknown but sometime between 24th and 28th of November 2009, Shari entered the couple's bedroom and fired the gun at Dwight Tobyne. It is presumed that she shot him in the head.

She then wrapped his lifeless body into the carpet that was already soaking up the blood and dragged him to a garage where she proceeded to chop his corpse into pieces. She took her time with each and every part, first cutting off the arms and feet. She did use a saw, as well as some other tools, but Shari also tore away some pieces herself. The garage was a mess and she needed to get rid of every single evidence that could connect her to the murder.

After wrapping the parts into cellophane and carpet cutouts, she loaded them up in her car and started making rounds through adjacent counties, dropping them in remote areas by an interstate. She did her best to leave them a bit away from the road in hopes that the animals would drag the parts even further into the wilderness. She was certain that this was the way to keep the police off her trail and ensure that she will not get caught. She then cleaned the crime scene with plenty of bleach, removing each and every spec of blood from the floor and walls. She presumably got rid of the saw and other tools as well.

She kept Dwight's cell phone and intended to pretend like he simply left her. She planned to contact her children every now and then via text messages and e-mails so they would think that Dwight was alive and well, soaking up the sun in Mexico. Since Shari wouldn't make any profit from her husband's death, the only explanation was that this was a crime of passion. They were married for almost thirty-five years and Dwight simply couldn't leave her right then after everything they went through. Shari's emotions obviously get the best of her and the result was gruesome.

The discovery of the crime

Even though Dwight missed the Thanksgiving dinner, the biggest red flag was the fact that he wasn't present at the birth of the Tobyne's second grandchild. He did contact his children via text messages so they though he was alive and well. But when he didn't show up at the hospital, his oldest daughter alerted the police. It was July of 2010 and the law enforcement immediately started working on this case.

The Tobyne children told the authorities that their father wanted to move to Oklahoma but their mother told them that he went to Mexico. The investigators were certain that the story was false so they focused their attention on Shari since she was the last known person to see him alive. She was living with her children at the time because she had to move out from the condo she shared with her husband and didn't have enough money to support herself on her own. When they brought Shari for the first interview, she denied everything. Shari told them that she had no idea where her husband was at the moment and that he hadn't contacted her in months.

She was released but the police investigators did sense that something was very wrong with her statements. They decided to put her under surveillance in order to see what she would do next and monitor any possible suspicious activities. Just like it was expected, Shari started acting oddly. The police officers saw her disposing of something in a dumpster and when they got there, they discovered a couple of clothing items, as well as pieces of a gun. She then proceeded to clean the trunk of her car which was even more alarming to the detectives because it looked like she was getting rid of the possible evidence.

Then they managed to locate Dwight's Ford pickup truck at a parking lot. It was obvious that the car was there for months but no one had reported it because it was parked in front of a residential building and there were a lot of vehicles there on a daily basis. There was no physical evidence of the crime anywhere in the car which meant that Shari probably didn't use it for body disposal. Checking the cell phone records was the next step and the investigators discovered that both of their phones were at the same location during the time frame when the possible murder occurred, as well as afterward. So Shari's story about Dwight leaving for Mexico in November of 2009 was clearly false because he wouldn't leave his phone behind. It was time to bring her back to the station for a second interview.

Shari broke down under pressure and told the detectives a whole new story. She said that she bought the gun with an intention to use in for her own suicide. Shari was feeling horrible after everything she had done with her husband's money and she wanted to end her life. The fact that Dwight was leaving her added to her depression and she simply couldn't continue to live anymore.

She brought the gun to their bedroom wanting to shoot herself in the head. Instead, Dwight who was there as well noticed the gun, grabbed it from her hands and unintentionally pulled the trigger while they were fighting for the weapon. He shot himself and was losing a lot of blood quickly. He was soon dead. Shari then said that she was lost and scared, knowing that no one would believe her story. So she quickly wrapped her husband in the sheets and dragged him to her car. She drove off to a remote location and left his body there.

Shari insisted that the death was an accident and that she didn't mean to hurt her husband. She volunteered to take the investigators to the place where she dumped the body. Listening to her directions, they went east of Scottsdale and started combing through the area. They couldn't find any traces of Dwight's corpse even though they covered a wide field around the alleged dump site. They knew that a lot of time has passed since the killing and that animals could have dragged the body someplace else, but they couldn't find anything that could indicate that a corpse was there in the first place.

The investigators placed Shari in the jail and continued to question other possible witnesses that could shed some light on this case. It was obvious that Shari's story was either incomplete or entirely false. They approached the owner of the apartment which Tobyne's were renting at the time of the murder. She told the police that the carpet in the master bedroom was brand new after Shari left the condo and that she also noticed a strong smell of bleach in the garage. It was a minor clue at the time because the investigators knew that Shari was an obsessive cleaner and she would often go around the house with pure bleach in order to disinfect all the surfaces. However, once they put the pieces back together, the bleach will play an important part in the investigation because it was used to clean up the scene.

Finding Dwight Tobyne

Back in December of 2009, prior to the missing person report which was filed by Dwight's children, dismembered body parts were found near a highway in Pinal County, namely legs without feet. The cuts were partially clean but they could see that the murderer did apply some force and they were more focused on tearing off the limbs than on keeping everything pristine. The police officers were sure that a saw of some kind was used in the process. The parts were collected by the police and sent for further analysis. The second set of body parts was discovered in La Paz County only a couple of days later. Hikers bumped onto a man's torso near the main road and alerted the authorities who once again collected the evidence.

Two police departments got into contact and they examined their findings in order to determine that the parts belonged to the same person. And then, three days later, a person traveling on a motorbike noticed something strange on the side of the road near Sugarloaf exit. The authorities in the area were already aware that they had a dismembered body on their hands and the remains were transported to Pinal County to make sure they also came from the same victim. The results were positive but the identity of the man was still unknown because they hadn't found the hands so fingerprint search was out of the question. As a matter of fact, some remains are still missing to this day.

The investigators who were working on Dwight Tobyne's case were aware of the mystery man who was found in three counties and they took a DNA swab from his parents in order to see if it was the match. The dates of the discoveries overlapped their murder theory and the detectives feared the worst. But before they delivered it to the medical examiner's office, they compared Dwight's physical description with the collected body parts. Hugh Lockerby, a detective from Scottsdale who worked on this case said: "A left leg was recovered first. A couple of days later, north of Phoenix, right leg was discovered. One hundred miles west of Phoenix a complete torso was uncovered. I asked could they give me a little description of the race, the height, the weight, and I am listening as they are telling me this and that is the exact description of Dwight Tobyne."

When the tests came back positive, they confirmed that it was, in fact, Dwight Tobyne. Since Shari Tobyne didn't mention any dismemberment of the body in her second statement, they had enough evidence to prove that she was lying. It was time to confront her and try to find out what exactly happened on that fatal night in November of 2009.

Shari pleaded not guilty in front of a judge and repeated her story about the accidental shooting. Her lawyer, Anne Phillips asked the judge to allow a psychological evaluation of her client because she was impossible to communicate with. She refused to provide her with any helpful details and Phillips thought that Shari might need some psychological help due to the fact that she was suicidal in the past.

Her attorney also wanted to be sure that Shari Tobyne did understand the charges properly. It looked like she was not fully there and her responses were sparse, providing Phillips with short answers only. The judge allowed a psychiatric examination and it was confirmed that Shari was responsive and aware of her actions. She didn't suffer from psychosis or depression. There were no underlying psychological issues and she was capable of attending her own trial.

However, the way she acted after the murder told the psychiatrist who conducted the evaluation that Shari Tobyne was a textbook sociopath. Not every person has the ability to separate their emotions and continue acting normally after a crime like this. She was sticking to her story no matter how unlikely it sounded and it seemed like Shari did really believe in her version of the shooting.

The trial

As previously mentioned, Shari Tobyne pleaded not guilty in the initial hearing. The state had a solid case against her even though they had no witnesses to the murder itself. She did confess to accidental shooting so she clearly was involved to some degree. However, her actions after the gun went off told a different story about a very violent body dismemberment and disposal. The fact that Shari lied to the authorities about the location of the body dump added a whole new layer to the case. She obviously didn't want the body to be found and hoped that the animals would do the dirty work for her.

Shari was facing the charges of a first-degree murder, as well as a concealment of the body parts. Since she did have some sketchy history regarding the financial fraud, the authorities had enough evidence to add it to the charges as well. They were asking for the death penalty. Shari's attorney didn't have much to work with but she repeated her old story about the accidental shooting. The verdict could have gone in both ways at that point, depending on the jury. So instead of going on a trial, Shari decided to end it as quickly as possible.

Shari Tobyne pleaded guilty on May 19th, 2012, ending the trial. It was the only way she could avoid the death penalty. That was a clever decision because her claims were simply not strong enough to convince everyone that she didn't shoot her husband on purpose. So instead she received life in prison and an additional thirty-one years for the financial fraud.

The children were in shock from the beginning of this case and they had a difficult time accepting the fact that their loving mother could actually kill their father. Shari Tobyne remains behind the bars and it is unclear when and if she would get an opportunity for an appeal.

HUSBAND KILLER : THE TRUE STORY OF MARY WINKLER

26

JAMES FALCON

The Case of Mary Winkler

Mary Winkler, at first appearances, would seem to be an altogether normal woman. So too did her family, with a husband who was a Church minister and three young children, girls aged just eight, six and one.

The family lived in Selmer, Tenn., a small town occupied by around 4,500 people, according to the 2015 census. The town is situated to the south west of the state. Not much has happened in Selmer; the most famous person to have been born there was Chad Harville, former pitcher for the Oakland A's, and for one year, the Red Sox. He achieved a 4-9 win-loss record over his career in the MLB.

Today, the most famous- or infamous- person to have come from Selmer is Mary Winkler. In 2006, Mary sparked a border-crossing manhunt, and a court case followed nationwide. She had killed her husband with a shot to the back from the family's shotgun. But it was the gripping, and at times bizarre, court case which gripped the attention of the nation.

Matthew dead, Mary and the family Missing

The date was March 6th, 2007. It was a Tuesday like any other. Mary and Matthew were at home all day together, although Matthew was due to give a sermon that evening.

It was actually members of Matthew's congregation who found his body that night. They had visited his home to check up on him after he had missed the service he was set to give; instead, they found him lying dead, having been shot in the back.

There was no sign of Mary or any of their children at the home, and as such, they were reported missing. The authorities quickly sent out an Amber Alert, since nobody had any idea what could have happened to them, or where they might be. Family and friends had no information to provide police on their whereabouts.

There was every chance that the family had been kidnapped or murdered, and their bodies disposed of elsewhere, although police could not identify a break in, and had no reason to believe that anything of value had been stolen.

It was only a day later that she was arrested in Alabama, having run from the family home with her young children. They were found 350 miles away from home, at Orange Beach, and in the back seat of the van was the family's shotgun. It was certainly suspicious; but what reason could Mary have possibly had for committing such a crime?

The Trial

In the build up to the case going to trial, public interest ramped up. Speculation had been rife about why Mary would have murdered her husband, a seemingly nice, well respected member of the local community. Perhaps either one of them had had an affair, and Matthew had been killed in a crime of passion. Or maybe he had been killed for an insurance claim?

As such, the press reported every step of the story as it came out during the hearing. The trial began when a Tennessee Bureau of Investigation Agent John Mehr read a statement that Mary had made very soon after her arrest. In it, Mary claimed that the couple had been arguing about their family finances, before Mary had shot her husband with their 12 gauge shotgun. She had said that the last thing she had wanted was to actually murder her husband, but she had been brandishing the gun in an effort to convince him to work through their problems, together. The argument had been ongoing throughout the day, and Mary had finally snapped, resorting to drastic measures to be able to convince him. She had never intended to kill him: she had said in the statement, 'I don't want this at all. I don't want any of this to be, at all.'

The statement continued on, and Mary claimed that they had argued often and argued fiercely. 'He had really been on me lately,' Mary had said, 'criticizing me for things- the way I walk, I eat, everything. It was just building up to a point. I was tired of it. I guess I got to a point and snapped.'

At first glance, it would seem that Mary had simply lost her composure, become angry, and killed her husband 'as the red mist had descended'. But after their initial statement, Mary's attorney indicated that there was much more that would come out about Matthew's behaviour when she testified which would help to explain her actions. Clearly, there were more problems with their marriage than the occasional, albeit fierce, argument.

Mary's Crime

The case for the prosecution wasted no time in painting Mary as a cold blooded killer, who left her husband to die without remorse. Admittedly, the plain facts of the case made Mary seem unbelievably guilty. The prosecution relied on several of these facts in their attempt to convince the jury of Mary's guilt for the charge of murder.

Mary had disconnected the phone immediately after she shot her husband, stopping him from being able to call the emergency services, or receive any calls that may have come in. This suggested that Mary had been in full control of her actions, not panicking, since it is unlikely that somebody in a state of anxiety would think to disconnect the phone.

The fact that Mary had attempted to flee to Orange Beach, Alabama, was also a key point for the prosecution. Immediately after Matthew's death, Mary had taken the family minivan to the beach, with her three children. Later on in her defence, Mary would claim that she ran because '[n]obody would believe me, and they'd take the girls away and put me away.' Certainly, in many murder cases, the fact that the defendant flees the scene is a certain indicator of guilt.

The family's daughter Patricia testified that she couldn't understand her mother's actions. All that she knew was that she had heard a 'big boom', and the sound of something heavy hitting the floor. She quickly ran to the bedroom to see her father on the floor, and her mother holding the shotgun. She had no idea what could possibly have provoked her mother to shoot him.

Another sticking point was that the family finances had been 'in shambles' just before the murder had taken place. This had led Mary to become embroiled in what is called a 'check kiting' scam. In it, she had received checks from unidentified accounts in Canada and Nigeria, and had ultimately fallen to a financial scam that had lost the family money. Prosecutors claimed that this could have somehow instigated the argument that led to Matthew's death, and that Mary had felt as if she had no way out of the scam.

They also jumped on the fact that in an initial conversation with investigators, Mary had told them that their marriage was a happy one, and that '[t]here's no poor me. I'm in control.' They clearly wanted to paint a picture of Mary as remorseless, deceitful, and smarter than she looked.

The Cross-examination

During her cross-examination in court, Mary stated that she didn't remember grabbing the gun from the closet in which it was kept. What she did remember was that 'something went off', 'hearing a loud boom', and that 'it wasn't as loud as I thought it would be.' She did admit that she had shot her husband. Matthew rolled from the bed- upon which he had been lying as they had argued- and dropped to the floor. Mary described smelling gunpowder.

Prosecutor Walter Freeland asked her whether she understood that 'pulling a trigger is what makes it go boom', to which she replied that she did.

Matthew asked her why she had snapped and shot him. She could only say 'I'm sorry.' The shotgun blast had been inflicted from behind, directly into Matthew's back, and had caused severe damage to his organs and spine. According to prosecutors, he had in fact still been alive as Mary had run from the house.

But these simple facts were far from the end of the story, as Mary was to reveal.

Appearances and Revelations

At first, Mary spoke of her husband not in the past tense, but in the present, as if she couldn't quite understand how final her actions really had been. In reminiscing about happier times, Mary told the court that her husband was an intelligent, social man, and that the family had shared many 'good times' together. She also seemed to enjoy talking about her children, and the happiness they brought her.

This happy family life, however, was simply one side of the marriage. Mary's attorney stated that '[w]hat went on behind their closed doors is going to have to be told ... Some of what we've got from the state of Tennessee touches on sexual abuse.' Their defence was that Matthew had made Mary's life a 'living hell': '[w]e will show you proof that he would destroy objects that she loved, he would isolate her from her family and he would abuse her not just verbally, not just emotional and not just physically—in other ways, too.'

Just before the murder, Mary claimed that Matthew had been threatening their children and even attempted to throttle their infant daughter, Breanna. He had been shouting, angry, because he had wanted a son. As the case went on, it became obvious that this was only the tip of the iceberg, however, and more and more sordid details of their home life would come to light.

Matthew, Mary claimed, was a violent, abusive husband. Shortly after their marriage, he ordered her to stop socialising with any of her family and friends (a common tactic among abusive spouses in order to further isolate their partners from potential help). Winkler's sisters described how Mary seemed stuck in her marriage, unhappy, but unable to leave. In an interview, they said that 'As the years went on, she seemed to be nervous to show love towards us.'

Mary was commonly 'screamed and hollered' at by her husband. 'He just flailed. He's a big guy and he was just all over ... He'd point his finger inches away from my nose. Whatever he was upset about, it was my fault,' Mary had said. It could be over anything: 'I was fat, my hair wasn't right, the girls, if something went wrong, it was my fault. I didn't know when it was coming.' Mary described her situation as one familiar to abused wives and husbands across America.

Her attorney, Steve Farese, provided further information based on his conversations with Mary. She had needed her husband's permission for everything, even for getting her hair cut. 'This was constant, and she lived a life where she walked on eggshells.' This abuse, he said, had given Mary symptoms of post traumatic stress disorder, simply because 'she didn't know what was going to happen next.' Furthermore, a psychologist testified as part of Mary's defence, saying that her symptoms were those of clinical depression and PTSD.

During her time on the stand, Mary also claimed that Matthew had forced her to watch pornography with him, and that he had bought her several 'slutty' costumes for sex, which she normally would never have worn, but for fear of her husband. If she refused, Matthew wouldn't hesitate to get physical, hitting her or even using his belt to whip her. Mary famously produced a wig and a pair of white high heels in the witness box during her cross-examination to show the court evidence of Matthew's other side.

Mary stated that she was never happy watching pornography, dressing up in sexy outfits or performing the sex acts that Matthew wanted. She went along with his ideas, however, because she didn't dare face his reaction if she didn't. 'I'd just do anything to help him stay happy.' Throughout these revelations, Mary was visibly embarrassed and uncomfortable. Clearly she would have preferred that none of them had ever come to light; but Mary felt it necessary to brave what her neighbors, and the nation, might think in order to clear her name and justify her actions.

Mary's family had been quick to corroborate her side of the story. Her father, Clark Freeman, had spoken out through Good Morning America and detailed the 'physical, mental, verbal' abuse that his daughter had suffered. Other friends came forward during the court case, and gave similar verdicts on their relationship. A friend of Mary's,

Rudie Thomsen, said that '[o]ne Sunday, Mary came into the church and I looked at her and she had a black eye.' Similarly, Mary's friend Amy Redmon agreed that Matthew had been controlling: '[h]e was an authority figure, and he made the decisions basically. It was obvious.'

Conversely, Matthew's family denied that their son had been anything like Mary had depicted in her defence testimony. Matthew's father, Charles Daniel Winkler, said that his son was a kind, gentle man, who could have done nothing to justify what the defence was claiming. Diane spoke several times during the trial, lashing out at Mary: 'You've never told your girls you're sorry! Don't you think you at least owe them that?'

The dramatic story of a supposedly kindly, gentle church minister having such a sordid, cruel and abusive hidden life gripped America. The case was covered extensively on all major networks, discussed on late night panel shows

The Jury's Verdict

While the prosecutors had tried to convince the jury to convict her on a charge of first degree murder, they were unsuccessful. The jury came to their verdict by April, that year. It took them eight hours to deliberate their way to the decision; this mirrored the response of the nation, which was similarly undecided on just what punishment Mary really deserved.

Mary was found guilty of voluntary manslaughter, a charge which carries a far more lenient sentence than murder. While murderers can receive full life sentences, and in certain states receive the death penalty, the maximum sentence for voluntary manslaughter is only 6 years.

Mary showed little emotion at the verdict, but did embrace each of her relatives afterwards. In a show of support, her family had been sat in the row behind her, and all linked arms with one another to demonstrate their solidarity. Afterwards, she was taken back into custody to await sentencing.

Mary's attorney stated afterwards that Mary's testimony had been central in securing the more lenient sentence. 'I think Mary's testimony was integral in this decision. They had to hear it from Mary', Farese told the press. 'They judged her credibility and they saw that she had an abusive relationship and they made their judgment based upon that.'

For Mary, the most important implication of the verdict was that she could finally begin to think of being reunited with her children. Speaking on her behalf after the trial, Farese continued: 'We would like to do so many things to open up communication between Mary and the paternal grandparents and to get the children out of this cycle of constant upheaval over this terrible tragic event.' But the question of how long she would be in prison remained.

Mary's sentencing was scheduled for May 18th, at which point both Mary and the prosecution would have a final chance to address the court before the judge decided on the final jail term. However, the situation looked positive for Mary. Not only would the five months that she had been imprisoned awaiting trial be taken into consideration, but the judge had indicated that alternatives to incarceration would be on the table. Perhaps Mary could avoid jail time altogether.

Sentencing: The Trial at an End

Due to a scheduling error, the hearing took place around three weeks late, on June 8th.

Mary took to the stand one last time to plead for mercy. She read aloud from a prepared statement, telling Matthew's family of her sorrow and remorse for her actions. She was 'so sorry that this had happened', and would 'always miss and love' her husband. 'I ask for mercy and understanding, but I know whatever decision you reach today will be right ... I ask you to please let me go home today and be with my children.' Tabitha Freeman- Mary's sister- had also pleaded for leniency, in particular to let Mary be reunited with her children. She went as far as calling Mary 'the best example of a good person I can think of'.

Members of Matthew's family, too, took to the stand to plead their case for the prosecution. Charles and his wife were clearly hurt and in disbelief at Mary's actions both in murdering their son, and believed that Mary had purposefully smeared his name at trial. 'The monster that you have painted for the world to see? I don't think that monster existed,' Diane Winkler had said.

After speaking their pieces, all that Mary, her family, and Matthew's parents could do was wait until the judge's decision. The trial- as well as the very public 'trial' that Mary had been through in the media- was finally at an end.

The defence had requested that Mary be granted full probation, or judicial diversion, both outcomes which would have meant that Mary would spent no further time in prison, and even that her record would be cleared of wrongdoing altogether. This request was denied.

After recess, Mary was told that she would spend 3 years in prison for her crime. But Circuit Judge J. Weber McCraw reduced that amount to just 210 days total in prison before she would be allowed to leave on probation. She also had that sentence reduced further, due to the fact that she had spent five months incarcerated waiting for trial.

Moreover, that time would be spent not in jail, but in a mental health centre in Tennessee. There, she would receive treatment for both her depression and post traumatic stress disorder. After such a long ordeal, with the prosecution fighting to either put Mary on death row or to imprison her indefinitely, it seemed that she had gotten off with hardly a slap on the wrist.

Steve Farese branded the sentence 'a victory': '[s]he could be in prison for life, and that's what everybody thought she was headed for to begin with.' Her other attorney, Leslie Ballin, said '[s]he'll be able to get out and fight the battle she wants to, and that is to get her children back.' Mary could finally think about the future again.

But certain signs indicated that it would not be as easy to reconcile with her children and family as she might hope. Matthew's family left the courtroom without making a comment to the press, as did the prosecution, clearly disappointed in the verdict. They gave no indication that they would be happy to open dialogue about Mary's daughters- not with the woman whom they believed to have murdered their son in cold blood.

The aftermath of Mary's release

Mary was released on August 14th, 2007. She had only been sentenced the previous June.

Upon her release, her lawyer informed the press that Mary would not be speaking with them, to maintain her privacy. During her time in the mental health facility, Mary could finally begin her attempt to win full custody of her three daughters, and she was still fighting this case at the time of her release. She had not seen her children, apart from Patricia's brief testimony as part of the case, for over a year. Throughout the case, and after Mary's release, her children were staying with Matthew's family.

Moreover, she was still fighting a $2 million dollar civil lawsuit filed by Matthew's parents. They also took legal measures, which, if successful, would have meant that the custody of Mary's children remained with them.

After her release, Mary seemed happier to her family and friends. From an outside perspective, it could be easy to claim that this was just as much due to her happiness at avoiding a jail sentence as it was to her being rid of an abuser. She was in fact living with friends at first after her release, and went back to work at a dry cleaners in McMinnville, Tenn., 200 miles from Selmer.

In the same interview as was mentioned before, Mary's sisters agreed that she had changed entirely. After years of shyness, Mary seeming unable or unwilling to show love to them for fear of her husband's violence, she seemed to finally be able to open up. 'Now it's back to the old Mary [who] loves us and doesn't care to come and hug us and gives us a kiss on the cheek.'

Since then, Mary lived in McMinnville. She has moved between jobs, working at the dry cleaners, before starting work at a nursery. She briefly dated the brother of one of her most vocal supporters, Paul Pillow; afterwards, she moved in with Wayne Cantrell, a preacher living in Smithville nearby.

Mary regained custody of her three children in 2008, but by 2010, received the news that she had multiple sclerosis. Her diagnosis came at the worst time, as she was settling down in her new life; she had not long started medical school with the desire to become a nurse, and had to quit since the work would be too demanding. She hasn't returned to work since.

One comfort for Mary was that Matthew's parents seemed close to being able to forgive her. After her diagnosis, they gave Mary some time off from parenting by taking care of the children for a weekend, which soon turned into several months. Daniel Winkler has preached several times since the events on the topic of forgiveness, although when asked by local press why he chose the topic, he has refused to answer, presumably preferring to keep those details private.

Mary, too, preferred to put the past behind her. In an interview with WAFF 48, the NBC affiliate in Huntsville AL., she stated how she would prefer to stay out of the limelight, particularly for the sake of her girls. 'Whatever reason people have any problem with me, that's fine. Everybody's entitled to their opinion, but these girls are treated for who they are, not because of what their mother's done ... They're three very fine young ladies'.

Concluding Thoughts

Some members of the public reacted with disgust at the abnormally short sentence that Mary was given, and questioned whether a husband would have been given the same leniency as Mary was. Men's rights activist Glenn Sacks publicly questioned whether a man would have been shown such leniency, and pointed to the case of Scott Peterson (who received the death penalty for the murder of his pregnant wife) to indicate that no, a man would not. He also argued that the idea of abuse had been widened to include simple criticism, and should therefore not necessarily be used as defence of murder.

Conversely, there have been many women put in prison for murdering their abusive husbands, some for much longer than Mary Winkler. The 'battered woman defense', or the preferred terminology today of 'battering and its effects', is not a genuine legal defence in itself; it can, however, be used to convince a court of diminished responsibility. Its effectiveness is due to the sympathy that it elicits from jurors, who can be convinced that abuse is a form of provocation, and the murder a form of self defense. Under this defense, Mary's short sentence makes sense.

The case has remained a touch stone with regards to spousal abuse in the U.S. A made-for-TV movie, 'The Pastor's Wife', was released in 2011. It was based on the book of the same title, written by Dianne Fanning, an award winning crime writer. The story was changed somewhat, with the inclusion of a financial subplot involving tax fraud. However, it also made use of real life interviews with people who knew the Winklers- including Matthew's parents. His mother revealed that she could never believe Mary's story. Charles admitted that Mary's story could be true, and that he could forgive her if she confessed her purposeful intention to murder Matthew.

As for the community in which the family had lived, the reaction was largely one of forgiveness. According to members of that community, the town's 'Christian roots and ... its tendency to give people the benefit of the doubt' meant that they took Mary at her word. Mary's quite life in McMinnville and Smithville similarly shows that the American public would rather leave her and her family alone after their painful ordeal.

TRACEY GRISSOM

Claiming to be a victim of rape and other abuses, a distraught Tracey Grissom would travel to her ex-husband Hunter's workplace and shoot him six times in the back, receiving a twenty-five-year life sentence for his murder.

Her defense attorney would argue that Tracey was motivated by post-traumatic stress disorder caused by her Hunter's constant abuse and sexual assaults. One jury member had even asked the judge to be lenient in her sentencing as they were not allowed to hear details of her Hunter's alleged abuses (beatings, rape, sodomy).

But what really happened in the years that led up to May 15th, 2012? Was she in fact the victim of years of abuse by a psychotic husband? Or did she want to cash in on his $100,000 life insurance policy?

INSTANT ATTRACTION

The couple would meet during a dinner party in 2003 in Tuscaloosa, Alabama. Tracey was twenty-one years old and going through a divorce. She had a son, James Michael, from the previous marriage.

Family and friends would describe the union as "love at first sight." Hunter was blown away by the young Tracey's blue eyes and facial beauty.

"For him, it was love at first sight," crime author William Phelps said. "She was gorgeous."

A whirlwind courtship would ensue and the couple would elope in 2004.

"In the beginning, it was good," Tracey told CBS' 48 hours. "We had a friendship. Just your normal, honeymoon phase marriage."

"He was fun," Tracey said. "And he was attractive."

Hunter was two years younger than Tracey, however, and his mother felt that he had jumped the gun too early in the relationship.

Her words proved to be prophetic as after only eight months into the marriage, the marriage went south.

According to Tracey, their marital problems began with Hunter's drug addiction.

"I had caught him smoking marijuana," Tracey said. "Doing illegal things could cause a problem and I couldn't risk losing my son over."

Tracey claimed that she threatened her new spouse with a divorce but Hunter gave her his word that he would stop with his drug use. She stated that the relationship improved and the decided to start a construction company together.

"I took out an equity line to start a company," Tracey said. "Which was Grissom Construction. It was all in my name."

Hunter specialized in building elaborate boat docks. He had an artistic eye and could do docks, stairs, and other accouterments. The business began to grow in short order.

"They're going to take on the world," Phelps said. "They're going to be entrepreneurs and they're gonna make it."

They then had a daughter of their own, Anna Grace. The child was a long time coming for the couple. They had been trying for a long time as Tracey had five miscarriages before Anna Grace was born.

"She was premature," Tracey recalled. "Her heart and lungs were not developed. A very stressful time."

Behind closed doors things were rocky. On the surface, however, things looked good. They had a young family and were making money.

"All-American family," Phelps said. "White-picket fence. The whole nine yards. Middle-class. Suburbia. Maybe the Prince Charming that she's been waiting for."

But again, this was only on the surface. Tracey harbored secrets of her own. One of which was her own addiction to prescription drugs.

"Psychologically, there's something going on here," Phelps said. "There's something going on behind those beautiful eyes and it ain't good."

Tracey would often turn on on the children, showing off her temper. Then she would turn on Hunter.

"This would cause friction in the marriage," Phelps said. "And where there's friction, there's fire."

SETTING THE STAGE

Tracey would later state that Hunter would "act strangely" shortly before she filed divorce. She was a registered nurse and gave him an over-the-counter drug test. According to her, Hunter tested posted for marijuana, Oxycontin, opiates, and methamphetamine.

Hunter would later be arrested for marijuana possession but his family would insist that he never did the harder drugs.

Tracey would file for divorce in the summer of 2010 after six years of marriage. According to her, this would prompt physical abuse from Hunter.

Hunter had to move out but their divorce agreement would allow him access to the home.

"In September of 2010," Tracey recalled. "That was the first time he physically hit me. It (the abuse) got progressively worse. He had made the comments that if I told anybody he would kill me. I believed him."

Hunter' co-workers and family members would have a different take on the situation, however. His co-workers remembered a time when she tracked him down at one of the jobs and made a scene.

"She's screaming, jumping on him," Hunter's co-worker said. "Said something about him having another girlfriend and used the expression about, 'You are mine. I'll kill you. I'll kill you. You are mine."

"She's borderline demonic," Hunter's mother said. " mean, I absolutely believe—that she is that troubled."

Hunter's family continued to believe that he did not abuse Tracey.

"He did not have an abusive, an angry bone in his body," Hunter's aunt Gina said. "In fact, we kind of laughed at him because he was too laid-back."

The divorce was finalized in October of 2010.

EVIDENCE OF ABUSE?

Loran Richards was the first of Tracey's friends to notice the minor injuries on her body. She would inquire about the bruises but the answers she received were always evasive. Seeing Tracey with a black eye, however, forced her to try and get more answers.

"I said, Tracey, you may have terrible luck," Richards recalled. "But nobody is so unlucky that they trip, fall down the stairs, and hit their face on a baseball in the eye socket. So don't give me a lame excuse. You don't have to give me any excuse, but let's take a picture."

Tracey broke down. She gave her friend all of the grisly details, detailing the abuse she suffered at the hands of Hunter. Loran then became her advocate, taking pictures of Tracey's injuries. She would later state that she saw blood stains and other signs of abuse at Tracey's home.

THAT FATEFUL NIGHT

Now divorced, Hunter would arrive at Tracey's home on November 22nd, 2010.

According to Tracey, he then became enraged when Tracey told him that she had spent the night with a new lover.

"He told me that he was gonna kill me," Tracey recalled. Tracey stated that she tried to escape, running into the closet in order to "get away from the kids and to pray." Tracey's eleven-year-old son from a previous relationship was in the home as was the four-year-old daughter they have together.

Hunter caught up with her and knocked her to the ground. He tied a belt around her ankles and then began choking her.

Half-conscious, Tracey alleged to have been raped and sodomized.

The brutal attack would leave Tracey unconscious. She would wake up the next morning on the bathroom floor.

"I called Hunter," Tracey recalled. "I told him that I was bleeding and that I was hurt and that I needed help. And he told me, 'Fuck you. I hope you die."

Tracey wound up in the emergency room after the attack. Hospital records would show that she had a laceration on her head, bruises, and ligature marks on her feet.

Tracey would then be referred to the Turning Point domestic violence center.

Marian Waters would describe Tracey's injuries as among the worst she had ever seen in a twenty-year career.

Waters would testify that Tracey had suffered a horrific assault. She described her mental state as typical of someone who had just been raped; fearful, jumpy, fearing for her life.

Tracey had suffered a hematoma on her side that was the side of a grapefruit. She also claimed to have experienced rectal nerve damage which would require surgery as well as torn vaginal muscles requiring her to have a hysterectomy.

Police were called and Hunter would be arrested for rape, sodomy, kidnapping and domestic violence.

"And at that point, I feared for my life," Tracey recalled. "And I feared for my children's life."

A HIDDEN AGENDA

Hunter would be freed on bail but Tracey got a restraining order against him. She bought a gun and did not go anywhere unarmed.

She took photos of her injuries on the night of the alleged attack and texted them to Loran. Later, they would take more pictures.

Angered, Hunter would stop paying her spousal and child support. Tracey, however, may have had another scenario in mind for obtaining money.

She had forced Hunter to take out a $103,000 life insurance policy around the time their daughter was born.

On May 24, 2012, the day before Tracey shot Hunter, she would place a call to MetLife that was recorded.

"Thank you for calling MetLife, this is Pam. May I please have your name?"

"Tracey Grissom."

Tracey would then explain that she was angry that her husband stopped making payments on his policy. During their divorce proceedings, he had agreed to continue paying the premiums. Tracey stated she was calling to make sure that they had the correct address on file.

"Is there anything else I can do for you today?

"That's gonna be it!" Tracey said, hanging up.

"Well, May 14th was just like any other day," Tracey said, explaining the call to the insurance company. "However, I had moved four different times. Me and my children were running. We were running from Hunter. So I had called the company to let them know that they had my old address and to make an address change."

FALSE RAPE?

Shelly Standridge was hired by Hunter to defend him in the rape case. She would state that Hunter denied raping or even assaulting Tracey that night. Hunter did, however, admit to the fact that he and his wife had consensual sex that night...Rough consensual sex.

"So that night," Standridge said. "Hunter said that she was depressed and claiming she was going to kill herself. She was saying she wanted their relationship to work."

So she undressed in front of him. Her beauty was always impossible for Hunter to resist.

The two had sex despite Hunter having a new girlfriend at home.

Hunter's aunt, Gina, believed that Tracey wanted to kill Hunter before the rape case went to court.

"He had a new girlfriend, he was living with her," Phelps said. "He was moving on with his life. Hunter would claim that Tracey was jealous, obsessive, even stalked them."

"Hunter had moved on," Hunter's aunt said. "There was some court dates coming up that would prove that Hunter was innocent. There were court dates coming up that he would get visitation to his daughter. She had a lot to lose."

Tracey was on the anti-anxiety drug Klonopin. Hunter would tell his attorney that Tracey would take more than her prescribed dose. Because of this, she fell and cut her head. Hunter would then leave the house around 10:30 pm and go to his father's house. Tracey would call him hours later, at 3:20 am.

Hunter would state that Tracey had called to threaten him. She told him if he didn't want the responsibility of the children then she would make it where he would never be able to see them again.

Hunter's attorney did not know what Tracey's motive was for crying rape. She was very upset that he had a girlfriend.

MORE LIES...

Hunter would be arrested nearly twelve hours later, to his total shock.

Tracey would give her side of the story to the police which later is proven to be false.

She would tell police that Hunter had thrown her against the bathtub around 10 pm and claim to be unconscious until 4 am the next morning.

"But her phone records show she was on the phone all night, so she was never unconscious," Standridge said. "She was also using her data at 10:42 that night. She was using it again at 10:50 that night. ... She sends a text to her boyfriend at 1:49 am. She sends a text to her friend at 2:07 am. She sends another text to her boyfriend at 2:07 am."

Tracey would blame the calls on Hunter.

"All I do know is I was not the only person using my phone that night," Tracey said, suggesting that Hunter used her phone.

Medical records would show that Tracey's head wound was "purely superficial".

Only one suture was needed.

Furthermore, there was nothing on the medical record to support the fact that Tracey experienced vaginal and rectal tears. She did have bruises on her ankle and legs but the photos taken by police at the emergency room would not resemble the same photos that Tracey and her friend Loran would take days later. In the photos taken at the emergency room, an area of Tracey's body has no bruises. Days later, there is discoloration.

Tracey's attorney would blame the discrepancy on "blood thinners" which would cause Tracey to bruise easily.

There was also a discrepancy in her phone records. She would take a photo of her inner thigh, a deep bruise. This area of her body was not photographed by police during her emergency room visit. But on December 9th, almost two weeks later, Tracey took a photo of her inner thigh with the deep bruise

"He (Hunter) told me that he would make it to where nobody would ever want me," Tracey said after a 2010 attack. "I didn't report it because I thought he would kill me."

THE FINAL STRAW

Tracey woke up pissed on May 15th, 2012.

Hunter had been ordered to pay $2,100 a month for the rest of his life. He was not complying with the court order claiming that he was "out of work."

Tracey stated that she was on her way to a job interview when she saw a Grissom Construction sign out of the corner of her eye.

She stated that her initial plan was to take a photograph of Hunter at the job site in order to show proof that he was working as part of her litigation.

"I was getting ready to take the picture and when I looked up he was standing almost directly towards the front of the boat trailer," Tracey said. "He was looking back directly at me. He had this face, that's like mean - just, I don't know how to describe it. I mean, I see it over and over like it's right there all the time. He flipped me the bird, which to me was kinda like, 'Yeah I'm workin. Screw you.' And at that point, I panicked. At that point, I didn't know what else to do except to defend myself."

Tracey started firing. The first shot hit Hunter in the arm. He started to run and she fired again repeatedly. One of the bullets punctured Hunter's heart and he died of massive internal bleeding.

William Dockery was working with Hunter and was an eyewitness to the shooting. Hunter had turned to Dockery before the shooting and told him to "call the law". Before Dockery could pick up his cell phone, Tracey had commenced shooting.

Tracey then pulled out her own cell phone and called the cops on herself. She tearfully described that she had just murdered her husband.

CONFESSION

Tracey told detectives exactly what was going through her mind when she came upon Hunter at the construction site.

"Tell me about what happened," the detective said. "What led up to...what's going on."

"In November of 2010, he beat me unconscious and raped me...and, and left me for dead....and, and I finally pressed charges against him and he told me that he would make my life a living hell...and that's what he's done."

"What, what happened this morning that led up to you going..."

"I was going to work and I saw him...and he's been claiming that he-he's not working. And, so I pulled in there to take a picture of him...cause it was the truck that's still in my name...and the boat that's still in my name...and the trailer that's still in my name...He just stared at me and flipped me off...and I just went in there and shot him...I just shot him, I shot him, and I shot him."

Tracey would be distraught and tearful during her interrogation room confession. A few weeks later, however, she would call the insurance company to let them know that Hunter had died.

"Well, I was actually calling because I didn't know what I needed to do ... Hunter passed away May 15th and I actually am going a court case right now because it was due to self-defense..."

Hunter's family went ballistic over this. Tracey would claim that she had no money but she continued to pay his life insurance premiums.

"Even through the times when she's screamin' that she's destitute and has no money ... she continued to pay life insurance premium," Hunter's mother said.

"I don't think my sister concocted a story," Tracey's sister said. "Just so she could get insurance money. ... But that's all they (the prosecution) had."

THE TRIAL

Tracey's allegations of rape and sodomy would not be allowed in court testimony. She was allowed, however, to detail the effects of Hunter's abuse on her were.

Taking the stand, Tracey would lift up her shirt in court and show herself wearing a colostomy bag. She stated that she had undergone several surgeries after her husband's daily rapes wherein she suffered permanent rectal and vaginal damage.

Hunter's family was then allowed to speak at the hearing.

"This tremendous loss has changed me," Hunter's mother, Melanie Garner said. "And I don't know how to change back."

Chloe, Hunter's sister, had a victim's services officer read her letter in court.

"Tracey is psychotic," Chloe wrote. "She is the most selfish person human being on this earth."

"Every mother should pray every night that your son doesn't fall in love with someone like Tracey," Hunter's aunt, Gina Grissom said. "There have been lots of allegations against Hunter. We've never believed anything that has come out of her (Tracey's) mouth."

His aunt then looked directly at Tracey.

"Hunter was proud of his name. Why would you still choose to use our name, and bring it down?" suggesting that if Tracey hated him so much why didn't she go revert to her maiden name after the divorce.

The jurors would find Tracey guilty of murder. She would be sentenced to twenty-five years in prison.

One of the jurors, Janice Kelly, would contact Grissom's attorney Warren Freeman the morning after the trial. She had remorse over her decision and said that she wouldn't have convicted her had they had the rapes and abuse allegations been introduced as evidence.

"I feel I made a mistake," Kelly said. "If I had to do it over again, we'd have had a hung jury. We didn't get her side. She did not get a fair trial."

"We voted to convict because there was no dispute that Tracey shot Hunter," the jury foreman wrote in a letter that was addressed in the courthouse. "Jurors didn't believe prosecutor claims that she did it in order to collect a life insurance policy. We felt the shooting was a crime of passion, not for financial gain and that she should be sentenced accordingly. I wish we had seen evidence of the rape allegation. We feel that she just 'lost it.'"

"It's not fair, it's not fair!" Tracey sobbed as she was led out of the courthouse and to jail.

"We think the sentencing was too harsh," Tracey's attorney Warren Freeman said. "Considering you have the foreperson of the jury actually saying, we don't feel like she should be punished according to being found guilty of murder. Let's just say that there will be a basis for a new trial, and part of it will be something that the jurors saw that they weren't supposed to see and I'm going to just leave it at that until I file my motion."

"My son died running for his life," Hunter's mother said. "I don't know what was running through his mind but I hear him say 'momma.'"

"People who think that I murdered him in cold blood," Tracey said. "Either don't know the whole story or don't know everything that's happened.

Tracey was asked on CBS' 48 hours if she regretted pulling the trigger on that fateful day.

"No," she said flatly. "Because if I hadn't I would be dead. I truly believe that."

"She has a way of making everything she does look right," Hunter's aunt, Gina scoffed.

WITCH KILLERS : THE TRUE STORY OF SUZAN AND MICHAEL CARSON

TAMMY BENNETT

"What started as two hippies going on an acid trip that quickly evolved into a serial killing couple. Suzan thought that she was giving a vision by Allah. She could go on to kill homosexuals and witches. The two then imagined themselves to be these heroic martyrs battling the forces of evil. They were nothing more than schizophrenic killers."

"Oh God!"

"Sir, what is the address?" the police dispatcher asked for the second time.

"She's dead. There's blood everywhere. Everywhere."

The panicked landlord had just discovered the body of his tenant in her basement apartment in San Francisco. She was lying face down in a pool of blood, covered by a blanket.

Her name was Keryn Barnes. Twenty-three years old with long blonde hair and wholesome features that looked like someone you would meet at a church social.

The landlord had enlisted the aid of a plumber to go investigate the basement apartment he owned on Schrader Street in San Francisco. He had not heard or seen the lovely young woman that he had rented the place out to and was worried about her.

His worst fears would soon become realized.

Police would find no signs of forced entry and Keryn still had money in her purse. She did not appear to have been raped.

Keryn had sustained several blows to the head which caused a skull fracture. The coroner found a bloodied iron skillet in the kitchen cabinet and upon further examination determined that the young woman suffered twelve to thirteen stab wounds to the neck and face.

The apartment wall was painted with mysterious religious symbols, spiral shaped ankhs, triangles and other arcane drawings.

On the bottom of one wall, however, netted one clue.

The name "Suzan" was scrawled in black ink.

Police would go on to interview some of Keryn Barnes' friends and they would find out that the young woman had taken in a strange couple by the name of Michael and Suzan Bear. Keryn had met the two hippies at a party in the Haight-Ashbury district, becoming immediate friends.

"I know something about you," Suzanne said to the young Keryn. "You're anxious. You're curious. I know because I used to be like you. You know, searching. But Michael and I we got something, man. All you have to do is sit still. Sit still and let the power of the universe flow inside you."

Keryn listened in rapt attention as the older woman passed the joint to her.

"That's right," Michael said, eyeballing the blonde beauty in front of him. She was younger than Suzan but he could not bring himself to lust after another woman. Or could he? "This culture we live in, our minds and bodies have become disconnected. There's a whole conspiracy to set minds apart from our true selves. Mind and body have to be one. We have to fight against all of the evil forces that prevent that from happening."

Barnes loved the counterculture of the San Francisco scene and felt a kinship with the weird couple. These were the kind of people she wanted to meet, so different from the people she grew up in Georgia. They had their own belief systems and were not constrained by polite society.

In her eyes, they were "cool."

The Bears would talk to Keryn about transcendental meditation, psychic phenomena and their own interpretation of the Muslim religion in which the young woman found fascinating. The two hippies needed a place "to crash for a little while" and Keryn took pity on the duo, allowing them to stay with her.

She slowly became drawn into their way of thinking, becoming their acolyte but having no idea how dangerous they really were.

The Bears had no criminal record but they were about to embark on a murder spree in which they would avoid capture for over two years.

And Keryn Barnes would be their first victim.

SUZAN CARSON

On the surface, Suzanne Carson lived an otherwise normal life growing up in Arizona in the 1950s. Her father was a newspaper executive while her mother was a housewife. As she grew older, however, she became more reclusive. She truly believed she was psychic and because of her introverted nature she had very few friends. Suzanne did very poorly in school, suffering from severe dyslexia.

Suzanne would marry, becoming a housewife just like her own mother. She lived in Scottsdale but she did not put on the false front of being happily married. She had a teenage son and often flirted with his friends.

She had the life of privilege, her husband was wealthy and she would spend her afternoons playing tennis. In the end, however, Suzanne was accustomed to the wealth from both her upbringing and now her marriage. She wanted something more. She wanted power, authority and attention.

A sexual predator, she played the role of "Mrs.Robinson" to her son's high school classmates, shamelessly flirting and going out on "dates" with them. In later interviews, she would brag that she bedded "over one-hundred fifty" of her son's classmates. These sexual rendezvous were intensified with her use of hallucinogenic drugs (acid, peyote, hash, marijuana).

Suzanne went on an acid trip with one of her son's high school friends then woke up in the morning to find her entire living room painted in red triangles with the name "Suzan" written at the bottom. Not remembering what she did the previous evening, Suzanne claimed that there was "a hole in my head" and that "all of the electricity in the house" was now flowing through her.

Suffering from these delusions, Suzanne would describe her own visual hallucinations.

"Suzanne was a schizophrenic," forensic psychologist Paula Flowers said. "It grew worse as she got older and she obviously needed psychiatric assistance. She needed to have been diagnosed, medicated and perhaps even institutionalized. But this was the early 1980s and we didn't have a lot of the mental health precautions in place like we have now. She was, in essence, a functional schizophrenic. The people she came in contact with would write off her strange ramblings as coming from someone who was a 'bit off'. And when she moved to San Francisco she fit right in."

"We can argue that Suzanne may have been medicating herself with the daily use of drugs," Flowers said. "Her use of hallucinogenic drugs increased as the years went on. She would have 'visions' as she would call them but a doctor would call them delusions and consider her to be very, very dangerous. When you combine acid tripping with schizophrenia you can get a lethal cocktail and that is what we got with Suzan. The drugs would only enhance her bizarre visions and make things much worse."

Suzan grew tired of the role as a housewife while her husband grew tired of her bizarre thought processes and behavior. Her husband would divorce her and take his two children with him. She was now free to embrace the counterculture and free love philosophy that she always wanted.

She began developing her own radical interpretation of the Islamic religion and with her new found identity she changed her name from Suzanne to Suzan, thinking that the mess she created in the living room was some kind of sign from Allah.

Suzan took bits and pieces from the Islamic religion to fit her own needs as she enjoyed mescaline and marijuana. Square jawed and wild eyed, Suzan began losing her physical attractiveness and noticed that the teenage boys no longer paid too much attention to her.

She needed a new man.

Around the age of 35, she went through a serious acid trip and began to have visions. These visions called for her to have a spiritual partner to "complete her destiny".

She would meet this man in James Carson.

JAMES CARSON

James Carson was born in 1950 in Oklahoma. He grew up in a normal middle class family. His father was an oil engineer while his mother was a schoolteacher.

His childhood was typical until he was diagnosed with a rare bone disorder when he was very young. He was put on bed rest for several years where he devoured books of philosophy, religion, politics and history.

He grew to have a combative personality, however, regularly using drugs and alcohol.

"Part of James' mental illness was that he thought everyone was about to get him," Flowers said. "There would be no way in hell he could hold down a job. He was anti-social and argumentative, willing to take offense at the most minor details."

James would take a stab at normalcy, however, as he would meet a woman named Lynn at the University of Iowa where he obtained a masters degree in Chinese studies. The couple married, had a child, then moved to Arizona.

His wife worked while James stayed at home to take care of his young daughter. He was a loving father but his anti-social tendencies ran deep. He hated the government, believed in conspiracies and soon became impossible to live with. Lynn divorced James and soon afterward he met Suzan.

Long-haired and bearded, James cut a Charles Manson-esque appearance. His eyes were empty and soulless, often greeting people with an expressionless glare.

CRAZY AND CRAZIER

When the two first met at a party, there was instant chemistry. Suzan was nine years older, taking on the mother/God role that James seemed to be looking for. He loved Buddhist philosophy and had been waiting his whole life for a woman like Suzan, someone who turned her back on mainstream American values. Suzan liked younger men, she liked being looked upon as a mother figure, a spiritual guide that led young men into drug-crazed nights where she was the center of their world.

Suzan was looking for someone to worship her and she found that in James who made her feel sexually attractive again.

"They both described their meeting as instant electric attraction," Jenn Carson said, the daughter of James. "From that very moment that they met, they were just joined like magnets."

"Me and you," Suzan said meeting James for the first time. "We're the same."

"That right?"

"There is a defiance in you. You are who you are and you are going to stick to your guns. We're the same, you and I. There is a whole world out there that is trying to suffocate who we are. We can fight back. We can take our swords into battle together."

Suzan saw James as a reflection of who she was and the two begin a daily routine of pot, alcohol and hallucinogenic drugs. They would have daily discussions on the problems of the world and how only they understood it.

James, in essence, becomes Suzan's follower in their cult of two. They both had the same spiritual fantasies and they both suffered from mental illness.

Baptizing James into her self-made religion, Suzan decided that he should change his name. She christened him as "Michael", in reference to the archangel from the Bible who fought demons. They adopt the last name of "Bear" as James may have used his childhood fascination with the animals as inspiration.

"What we see happening is a reinvention of themselves," Flowers said. "By taking on these new identities they shed all of the ghosts of their past. Renaming themselves was a symbolic gesture, their way of taking control and being rid of the societal forces that they felt were keeping them down. They were free to recreate a new person and that person would have power. That person would be special, given a license from God himself to go and rid the world of evil."

The couple would go on acid trips and engage in their own invented prayer sessions. They would talk in tongues, read from selected verses in the Koran and then indulge in yoga-inspired chants. Michael was well-versed in eastern religions but again followed Suzan's lead as she went from one discipline to another in her mescaline-fueled prayer sessions.

"My father had always been interested in very radical religious beliefs," Jenn Carson said. "Those interests became more and more extreme."

"It was the most bizarre environment you can imagine. It was like being dropped into a rabbit hole. You have two individuals who both have mental health needs and now they're using very, very heavy drugs."

Suzanne would have visions, seeing kaleidoscopic lights through trees, strange elephant like creatures and ancient bronze statues with no form.

"Suzan truly believed that she was going crazy," Flowers said. "She had to recognize that her own brain was not functioning properly so perhaps that is why she believed that there was a divine entity that was telling her to commit these acts. She thought everyone was out to get them. The FBI was out to get them. A secret government agency was out to get them. Yet Allah is the force that is on their side."

Michael convinced her, however, that her delusions were a gift. Like an old time Biblical prophet, Suzanne was chosen to receive these visions from Allah.

"You're a prophet," Michael said with excitement. "You're a yogi. You're not a witch. You have been given privileged access. Your visions are a gift!"

"Maybe you're right," Suzan rubbed her head.

"There's a reason why Allah is invisible. Have you ever thought about that? No one else can see him. But you can hear him."

"There's a war coming," Suzan said. "God will send someone to fight the Evil. And that someone is us. That's what he's saying to me."

"That's right."

"Everyone will die," Suzan said, lowering her voice just in case someone from the government was listening. "Everyone who practices witchcraft. Homosexuals. Witches. All of the evil people. We have to look beyond ourselves. The police. The government. Celebrities and politicians. Every bad person will burn in fire!"

The vision fit in line with Michael's own paranoid schizophrenic personality. He saw witches everywhere, the government, the media, the person on the street.

Deluded and convinced of their own righteousness, they became a "cult" of two.

The duo would move to California for a new life, settling into the Haight-Ashbury district.

"They were on the hunt for new recruits," Flowers said. "I don't think they had clarity as to the type of person they were going for, male or female. They were simply looking for someone young and open-minded."

They would meet Keryn Barnes at the party and she would take the couple in.

"She (Keryn) was kind of interested in that eclectic scene," Jenn Carson said. "And she was very much a bohemian girl. When Suzan and Michael entered her life I think she found them fascinating."

"Keryn was young and impressionable," Flowers said. "She had embraced that whole San Francisco counterculture mentality where you do not judge anyone. She probably didn't see herself as a follower in their cult. She wanted some older people to hang out with, people who were different from her. She could not see what anyone in their right mind could see in Suzan and Michael. They were weird, crazy and dangerous."

Suzan, however, would grow jealous of the beauty of Keryn. She would notice the sideways glances that Michael would give the pretty and young Keryn.

"Suzan would look in the mirror and see an old lady with yellow teeth," Flowers said. "She wore no make-up and she had thick jawline with deepening wrinkles. She compared herself to the young Keryn and felt inferior."

Fearing that she would lose Michael, she began brainwashing her younger lover into believing that Keryn was a witch.

"Do you think she's pretty?" Suzan asked as Michael watch Keryn head into the bathroom.

"Yeah," he said, nodding his head without commitment.

"Keryn's a witch," Suzan said.

"No," Michael said. "Keryn is cool, man."

"She's siphoning away my youth," Suzan said. "Taking away my powers as a yogi. She's trying to come between us. I can feel it. She's doing it psychically. I know she is."

"What?"

"She's a witch. She must be dealt with."

"No."

"We have to kill the witch," Suzan said, looking deep her lover's eyes. "Michael, you have to kill Keryn."

"Suzan truly believed she had psychic powers," Flowers said. "She would look Michael directly in his eyes and try and communicate to him through telepathy. She thought she had ESP. He would always comply so his obedience would only provide further evidence that she did have psychic powers."

Repressing his growing lust for Keryn like any good religious disciple, Michael would obey his mother figure in Suzan.

On March 7th, 1981, Michael Bear Carson would kill Keryn Barnes, attacking her with a frying skillet as she slept on the floor.

He fractured her skill before stabbing her with a paring knife.

"Suzan and Michael portrayed Keryn as a witch," Jenn Carson said. "As a woman who was trying to break up a marriage. None of those things were true. This was a nice girl from Georgia. No one should go through what she went through. She was beautiful, delightful twenty-three year old girl."

"All of the crazy and deluded talk they have done has now come to a head," Flowers said. "They've just killed their first 'witch'. They both have delusions of grandeur in ridding the world of more 'witches', so away they go to kill as many 'witches' as they can."

Suzan and Michael then went on the run, heading toward Oregon.

They would find an isolated cabin in the woods and enjoy what they would call their own "private paradise". The anti-social couple were away from people and frolicked in the wilderness.

"This was meant to be," Suzan said, twirling around underneath the tall Oregon trees. "This is our reward for being good servants to Allah."

"This is true wealth," Michael said looking across the Oregon landscape, smelling the scent of the jasmine flowers. "Not something that you buy. It is contentment of the soul."

"We can stay here forever," she said. "But let us not forget that we are 'hash-ashins'. Islamic assassins. We must go out and search for more prey. There is still plenty of evil in the world. But this will be our refuge. Our safe-house."

Their delusions were short-lived, however, as the couple soon ran out of food and supplies in the cabin. Michael would hitch-hike into the nearest town where he met a local construction worker who let the couple stay in his tree house.

The man soon felt uncomfortable with the arrangement as Suzan said very little. She would laugh and smile at inappropriate moments. Suzan had a way of looking at a person, she would stare and then smile as if she knew something that the person didn't.

She gave him the creeps.

Sensing that the couple was dangerous, the man sent a thug armed with a gun to kick the couple out as they headed back to California.

They would find a marijuana plantation in California and land a job of care taking the illegal operation in a remote part of Humboldt County.

The couple did not make friends with anyone at the plantation and soon locked horns with a man named Clark Stevens who was part owner. Stevens could be gruff, not averse to four letter words and looked down on hired help hippies like Michael and Suzan.

Michael had an assigned post working security, standing guard at the fence in front of the hidden plantation. Stevens pulled up, honked his horn and demanded to be let into the farm.

"No one is supposed to be here today," Michael said, blocking the front gate as Stevens came out of his jeep.

"That right?" Stevens said. "Who the hell are you?"

"Who the hell are you?" Michael challenged back.

"I own this fucking place!" Stevens said. "Open the fucking gate."

"No," Suzan said. "Michael, you know you can't let him through. It is your job."

"Tell your bitch to shut up and open the fucking gate!" Stevens grew more agitated.

Suzan would see Stevens as a man that needed to be eliminated. Stevens would later criticize the way the hippie couple handled the plants and wanted them out off the plantation. The couple, however, decided to nip the flower in the bud and take care of Stevens themselves.

"He disrespected me," she said to Michael.

"What do you want me to do?"

"He touched me!" Suzan said, the words hissing from her mouth. "Are you going to let him get away with that?"

Suzan detailed a story in which she believed that Stevens had made a sexual pass at her. This gave Michael carte blanche to commit his murder.

Michael then confronted Stevens inside the plantation grounds and shot him in the head.

"Michael shot Stevens on the orders of Suzan," Flowers said. "She thought that Stevens had disrespected her and used Michael as her weapon of choice. That was part of her mental make-up, to use Michael as her hit man, so to speak. If she saw that someone needed eliminating she would snap her fingers and Michael would do her bidding. Disrespecting Suzan would be met with a death sentence."

The two then chopped up Stevens body, doused his body with kerosene and set him on fire.

"Just looking at the level of brutality," Flowers said. "The Stevens murder was a step beyond the Barnes murder with the added desecration of a dismemberment and burning of the corpse. The 'Witch Killers' weren't the type of serial murderers that had a set modus operandi. They were opportunistic and random which is what made them so hard to catch."

Police would later discover Stevens' body by accident when a helicopter spotted one of the dogs playing with what at first glance seemed like a ball.

Looking closer, they realized that the dog was playing with a human head.

The investigating police would later smell the body of Stevens before they saw it. His body had been only partially burned as the couple had covered him up with chicken manure which had been used to fertilize the marijuana plants.

KILLING RONALD REAGAN

The couple began making out a hit list of prominent figures they wanted to kill. At the top of the list stood Ronald Reagan and Johnny Carson.

The couple believed that the first, middle and last names had six letters. They saw supernatural significance in the numbers 666, the designation of the beast.

Still on the run, the couple would drive toward a roadblock. Police had blockaded the road looking for another criminal but the couple had mistakenly believed that the investigation was for them.

They stopped their stolen vehicle and immediately ran into the northern California woods. Deputies gave chase and would see Michael drop his backpack.

Inside his belongings, they would find his book which he titled "Cry For War."

"The book contained passages of Michael's philosophical beliefs," Flowers said. "Rambling on and on, it did attract interest of both the FBI and Secret Service, however, because the book wrote of assassinating the President. So now the deluded couple who imagined that big, black government helicopters were out to get them had to now face the real thing."

CAUGHT BY ACCIDENT

Michael would later be detained by police as he fit the description of a rapist. He had stolen some identification from someone else and gave the police that false information.

The police took his picture and faxed it over to the hospital so the rape victim could make a positive identification.

The victim said hat it wasn't him and Michael was released.

Taking to the road again, the couple began hitch-hiking. They were soon picked up by a man named John Hillyer.

"The couple now had more than a little blood lust in them," Flowers said. "They no longer limited themselves to killing people that they perceived as 'witches'. Now anyone that showed them the slightest amount of disrespect would be in mortal danger."

"You folks need a lift?" Hillyer called out.

Michael gave a thumbs up to the driver, moving toward the vehicle until Suzan stopped him. "He might be a witch," she said. "We're going to have to kill him."

The couple climbed into Hillyer's pick up truck. Suzan sat in between the two men. Hillyer played country music on the radio which Suzan hated.

"Witch music," she whispered.

Then Hillyer's leg accidentally brushed against hers.

Suzan interpreted the touch as a sexual pass. She looked at Michael, gazing deep into his eyes. Without saying a word, she tried to communicate to him through telepathy that he had to kill Hillyer.

Michael said nothing as he took out his gun.

"Hey man," Hillyer said. "What the hell is that?"

Michael hesitated. Then he pointed the gun at Hillyer.

Hillyer grabbed the gun and a struggle ensued. Suzan got into the middle of the fracas, scratching and clawing at the driver.

"The fuck is wrong with you people!" Hillyer screamed.

The fight for the gun continued for ten minutes, Hillyer trying to wrest the weapon away from Michael while Suzan screamed and bit him.

The car skidded to a stop on the highway.

Hillyer stepped out of vehicle, letting go of the gun.

There were witnesses. Surely, this crazed couple would not shoot him in broad daylight with all these people around who could identify them.

Hillyer attempted to sprint over to the side of the road.

"John jumped out to run for his life," Jenn Carson said. "And Suzan and Michael proceeded to both stab and shoot him on the side of the road in full view of commuters driving by. John died on the side of the road."

"John died because Suzan ordered it," Flowers said. "Michael was the willing patsy, a violent enabler, if you will. He did all these things to make her happy. Hillyer had innocently brushed his leg up against Suzan's. In Suzan's demented world, that was a capital offense."

The numerous witnesses, however, allowed the police to positively identify and capture the killers, ending their rampage.

MEDIA COVERAGE

In a bizarre twist, the couple held their own public news conference where they were allowed to detail their deluded philosophy. The two then went on a five-hour televised rant in which they justified their killings as a war on witchcraft.

"We rid the world of evil!" Suzan proclaimed. "Witches. People with dark forces."

"They did talk about the murders," Jenn Carson said. "And laid down this case that they were being spiritually attacked and that they had to defend themselves. That they were called to kill witches, their whole rationale."

The press conference was broadcast by KGO-TV in the San Francisco Bay Area.

"Their delusions were made public," Flowers said. "In hindsight, this really set a wrong precedent as it gave two deluded people a public stage. A part of me thinks that a defense attorney staged this in order to make the case that these two should not be able to competent to stand trial. If that was the case, it didn't work thankfully."

"In looking back, we see these two mentally ill people who were totally convinced in their psychotic beliefs. In their delusions of grandeur, they wanted the world to know of their work."

On June 4th, 1984, Suzan and Michael Carson were found guilty of the first degree murder of Keryn Barnes. Later, they were found guilty of the murders of Clark Stevens and John Hillyer.

Both were sentenced to a total of 75 years to life.

"Michael and Suzan were like dynamite and a match," Jenn Carson said. "Without the other, would this have occurred? I don't know."

Jenn Carson has now come to terms with her father being a serial killer.

"I would describe my father as brilliant," Jenn Carson recalled. "Handsome. Charming. Damaged. Misguided and soulless."

"I think Suzan is intelligent," Jenn Carson said. "And crazy. And evil."

"You absolutely cannot have rehabilitation when there is absolutely no remorse," Carson said. "Neither of these people feel any remorse whatsoever. They speak about it, in a way that almost glamorizes it, and Suzan has bragged about being friends with the Manson girls in prison. There doesn't seem to be any sign whatsoever that they would come out changed in any way."

James Carson is incarcerated at Mule Creek State Prison while Suzan is jailed at the Central California Women's Facility.

They were both up for parole in 2015, becoming eligible because of their age and prison overcrowding.

Both were denied.

The Crimes of The Papin Sisters

Amy Delaney

The Papin Sisters

Clémence Derré did not have the best reputation. She was well known for being promiscuous and was not a desirable candidate for Gustave Papin, whose parents disliked the girl, especially after finding out about her affair with her boss. She was the talk of the town, but Gustave was in love, and nothing anybody else could say or do would change his mind. Besides which, Clémence was pregnant with Gustave's baby, and Gustave wanted to do the right thing.

On October 3rd, 1901, Gustave Papin and Clémence Derré were married, and four months later on February 12th, 1902, their daughter Emilia was born.

However, things did not go the way Gustave had imagined. His young wife had absolutely no interest in either her new daughter, or in fact, her husband, and showed little affection to either.

Gustave's suspicions began to grow. Having steadfastly stood by Clémence when the town people had turned against her, he now began to believe that maybe the rumours had been true after all. He started to wonder if it was possible that his wife had not only had an affair with her boss but was still doing so.

Gustave made several attempts to catch his wife out – lying in wait whenever and wherever he thought they might be, but his efforts proved futile.

With his jealousy growing, Gustave decided that the only solution would be to move his wife and daughter away from the town altogether, taking Clémence out of temptation's way.

Gustave set about turning his plans into reality, and in July 1904 he secured himself a position at a saw mill in Marigné, 8km away, believing it to be a second chance for the couple. However, Clémence was furious – she had no desire to leave her home or her lover and reacted by threatening suicide. But by this time she was pregnant with the couple's second child, so she resigned herself to starting a new life in a new village, knowing that nobody else would want a pregnant woman.

On March 8th, 1905, their second child was born – another little girl whom they named Christine. But if Gustave was hoping for a reversal of the state of their marriage he was disappointed, as the relationship disintegrated even further.

Married life was not how Gustave imagined it to be – his wife complained bitterly about her constant tiredness and her unwillingness to look after their daughters, so Gustave took matters into his own hands, and sent Christine to live with his elder sister Isabelle, who also lived in Marigné.

In August 1910 Gustave and Clémence settled in Le Mans with their daughter Emilia, and on September 15th, 1911 Clémence gave birth again, to a third daughter whom they named Léa.[1]

Christine

Christine was happy at her Aunt Isabelle's. Isabelle had a deep mistrust of men but had always wanted to be a mother, so when she was given the opportunity to take in a baby to raise as her own, she jumped at the chance. Isabelle's own mother had been destroyed, at least in Isabelle's eyes, by numerous pregnancies, and she was adamant she was not going to go the same way. She had worked as a maid and when her elderly employer died, Isabelle was left a small inheritance. She was fiercely independent and greatly disapproved of Christine's mother for her various involvements with men. According to Isabelle, as long as a woman stayed away from men she would be safe.

But Christine absorbed her Aunt's hatred of men, and in turn developed her own distrust of them.

Rape

Sometime around Léa's birth, a shocking secret emerged. Clémence found out that her husband, Gustave, had raped their first born daughter, Emilia, who would have been only around ten at the time. Clémence reacted with fury, but she not only directed that fury at her husband but also at her daughter Emilia, whom Clémence believed had seduced Gustave. There was talk of Emilia not being Gustave's daughter, and Clémence assumed that the little girl had been a willing sexual partner to her father, and had enjoyed it.

Clémence took her revenge on both of them.

She divorced Gustave, as one would expect for such a heinous crime, but she also took revenge on Emilia, sending her away to a religious orphanage called Le Bon Pasteur. The orphanage had a reputation for harshness, and Clémence thought it might force her 'errant' daughter to mend her ways. At the same time, Clémence removed Christine from Isabelle's care and placed her alongside her sister at the orphanage. Baby Léa was given to a great-uncle to be looked after, and Clémence, now both husband and child free, obtained work as a maid.[2]

Léa

Léa stayed with her uncle until 1918, when she was around seven. When her uncle died, Clémence placed Léa into a religious institution in Le Mans[3], where she would stay until 1924.

Emilia

Not a lot is known about Emilia Papin, except that, after her time at Le Bon Pasteur, she decided to enter the convent and dedicate her life to the church. As far as records show, she spent the rest of her life there.[4]

Back to Christine

Christine was set to follow in her older sister's footsteps – she, too, wanted to join a convent. While she had had Emilia at Le Bon Pasteur with her, she had felt protected and loved, but with Emilia now in a convent, Christine found herself alone. The love she had felt for Emilia now had nowhere to go, as entering the convent no doubt meant excommunicating herself from her family. So Christine turned her affections towards her little sister, Léa.

Christine's plans were scuppered by Clémence, however. The woman had been furious when Emilia had joined the convent, as she had been getting to an age when she could go out to work and earn money to send to her mother. So when Christine decided she wanted the same life, Clémence put her foot down, exercising her parental rights.[5]

At that time, in France, the age of majority was 21, meaning that parents had the deciding say on what their children did up until that time. So Clémence, seeing her meal ticket disappearing the same way it had with Emilia, prevented Christine from joining a convent and instead committed her to a life of service.

Christine was well suited to the life of a maid – she had spent eight years at Le Bon Pasteur where she had been expertly taught in skills such as housekeeping and sewing.

Christine found work easily enough, but she was forced to leave several jobs because, according to her mother, the pay wasn't enough for her (Clémence's) needs.

When Léa was old enough, she too went into service, and the two sisters often worked together in the various homes of their employers.

The Lancelins

In 1926, when Christine was 22, she managed to secure a position with the Lancelin family in Le Mans.

René Lancelin was a retired lawyer, who lived at No. 6 rue Bruyère, with his wife, Léonie, and their grown-up daughter, Geneviève. The couple had another daughter who lived away from home.

When Christine had been working for the Lancelins for two months, she asked them if they would consider hiring Léa as well. Madame Lancelin was impressed with the standard of Christine's work, so she agreed to take on her younger sister too.

Life went on, with Christine working as the cook and Léa as the chambermaid. The girls were diligent with their work, putting in 12-14 hour days and working six and a half days a week. Their only time off was a half day on Sundays when the girls would attend church, dressed appropriately, with gloves and hats.

The sisters had no interests outside of each other and the church, apart from an occasional visit to a local medium, and the remainder of their time was spent in the attic room they shared. They showed no interest in meeting suitors, or dancing, or going to the movies.[6]

At first, it would seem that the sisters had a reasonable relationship with Madame Lancelin. When their employer found out that they were sending their wages to their mother, Clémence, she urged them to stop passing it on and keep it for themselves. She even went so far as to tell Clémence herself that her 'gravy train' had now stopped. The girls' wages were around 3000 francs per year, which amounts to around $2236 today.[7]

Because of Madame Lancelin's kindness, the sisters began referring to her as 'Maman' in private.

Although their living arrangements were basic – the sisters shared one small bed in the attic for instance – they had a balcony from which they could watch the people of Le Mans pass by. It was a relative luxury among the serving community.[8] Indeed, as servants go, the sisters had it better than most. There was always plenty to eat, and the girls had a heated bedroom, a luxury which many other servants of the time were denied.

The Tide Turns

After a few years, things began to take a downward turn in the Lancelin household. Although both the girls had an enviable reputation with regards to their work, their personalities seemed to cause some consternation among other people. Local shopkeepers found the girls to be aloof and reserved, and one woman, who herself had employed Christine for a couple of weeks, described her time with Christine as difficult, stating that she found the girl so touchy and rebellious that she was loath to ask her to do anything. Nonetheless, their professional standing was second to none – unlike other maids of the time, the sisters did not engage in any flirtations with local boys and applied themselves meticulously to their duties.

Despite Madame Lancelin's initial kindness in ensuring the girls got to keep their wages, she became an increasingly hard taskmaster and took to wearing white gloves to check that the sisters had left no dust anywhere.

Communication became stinted. Madame Lancelin would only communicate with Christine and not Léa, and even then it would invariably be via a typed message regarding their work rather than through actual conversation.

Monsieur Lancelin himself later admitted that he had never once spoken to Christine or Léa during their seven years of service in his house.[9]

Sisterly Love

The fact that the sisters spent so much time together alone in their room did not go unnoticed. Christine was also fiercely protective of Léa, and was apparently extremely jealous of Genevieve Lancelin, whenever she attempted to initiate conversation with the younger sister. On one of the girls' visits to the local medium, they had apparently been told that Christine had been Léa's husband in a past life, a belief which she seemed to act out. In fact, such was the abnormality of the closeness and affection the sisters shared for each other that Madame Lancelin and her family began to suspect that the two young women were engaged in sexual relations.[10]

The sisters were unnaturally close, described by some that knew them as obsessive. They would braid each other's hair, make clothes for each other, and spent every moment together, completely shunning any outside interests. On one occasion, Madame Lancelin took it upon herself to spy on the women and had her suspicions confirmed when she caught the sisters making love. One can only imagine the shock – at the time homosexuality was very much frowned upon, and when you add incest to the mix it became even more scandalous. To the girls, though, their behaviour probably felt completely normal. Their own father had raped their sister, and their Aunt had consistently warned against the perils of mixing with men.[11] Their father had disappeared from their lives after his sexual abuse of Emelia had come out, apparently fighting in World War One and subsequently re-marrying[12]) and they had found in each other the affection and love that their own mother had been unwilling or unable to provide. The love they had for each other was the only love they had ever truly known. Madame Lancelin decided to share what she had seen with the rest of her family, but for one reason or another no action was taken, and life carried on.

The situation became more strained after a particular incident involving Léa and Madame Lancelin. While cleaning the floor, Léa had missed a tiny scrap of paper, which Madame Lancelin noticed, and, enraged by the girl's inattention to detail, pinched Léa hard and viciously until she was forced to her knees to pick up the offending piece of paper. Léa, who was normally very quiet and withdrawn, told Christine *"She had better not try that again or I will defend myself."*[13]

Christine's Descent into Madness

Towards the end of 1932, Christine's behaviour began to change. She began to suffer explosive fits of anger which she directed at her younger sister, Léa. The previously loving, albeit unnatural, relationship became a frightening ordeal for the younger sister as she could do nothing but suffer her older sister's outbursts which came from nowhere. Her normally kind demeanour was slowly changing into that of someone totally alien to her.

The pair continued to perform their duties for the Lancelin family, but Christine was losing her grip on reality. She began to suffer from hallucinations – seeing and hearing things which were not there, and these episodes, which today would have been recognized as symptoms of paranoid schizophrenia, in turn, set off panic attacks in Léa, who could not cope with her sister's state of mind, and behaviour.

It was all about to come to a tragic and fatal head.

February 2nd, 1933

The late winter was making its presence felt in Le Mans on February 2nd, 1933. It was bitterly cold, and the wind was howling outside.[14] Madame Lancelin had spent the day shopping with her daughter, Genevieve, and the pair were due to meet Monsieur Lancelin at his brother in law's house for dinner later that evening. Christine and Léa were not expecting their employer home until late into the night.

One of Léa's jobs for that day had been to take a broken iron to the electrician's to be fixed. However, when she returned home and plugged it in ready to do some ironing, it shorted the power to the entire house. As the Lancelins weren't due home until late that night, Christine took the decision to leave fixing the fuse until the next morning.

However, Madame and Genevieve Lancelin did return home, sometime after 5.30 pm, and were annoyed to find the house in darkness. Christine met them at the door and explained that the iron had been fixed, but that when it had been plugged in it had shorted the power. Madame Lancelin was furious at this news and a row broke out.

It was enough to tip Christine over the edge.

The older sister grabbed a pewter jug and brought it down onto Madame Lancelin's head. Her daughter, Genevieve, heard the commotion and came rushing to her mother's aid, only to receive a similar blow. As Christine began to fight with Genevieve, Léa joined in, struggling with Madame Lancelin, who had managed to recover somewhat from the blow. As the fight continued in the darkness, Christine shouted: *"I'm going to massacre them."*

As the fight became more frenzied, Christine began to shout orders to her sister.

"Smash her head into the ground" and "tear her eyes out"!

Léa had always followed her older sister's orders, and she wasn't about to stop now. With her bare hands, she gouged Madame Lancelin's eyes out, while Christine did the same thing to Genevieve.

As the two women lay writhing, blind and in agony on the floor, the sisters went on the search for weapons with which to continue their brutal attack. Finding a knife and a hammer, they returned to the grisly scene, and systematically beat their employers with first the pewter jug, and then the hammer. Mercifully for the Lancelin women, death came at last. But, even though they could no longer feel it, their mutilation was far from over.

The Papin sisters then 'prepared' the bodies of the two women as if they were preparing a joint of meat for dinner, carving deep gashes into their flesh. Lifting the skirts of the two women over their heads, leaving them with no dignity whatsoever, the maids sliced into their thighs and buttocks. Their final act of humiliation was to smear Madame Lancelin's body with Genevieve's menstrual blood, basting her as they would baste a joint of beef.

The Discovery

While his wife and daughter were being slaughtered in their own home, Monsieur Lancelin was at first irritated, and then worried, when they failed to show up for dinner. He made the journey home to pick them up, but when he arrived he couldn't get in. The house was locked and bolted from the inside. He thought it strange that the maids hadn't answered the door, but decided that perhaps they hadn't heard him and that his wife and daughter had already left for Madame Lancelin's brother's house.

When he returned to his brother in law's house, however, there was still no sign of his wife or daughter, and Monsieur Lancelin began to worry. Enlisting the help of a dinner guest, he returned once more to his house, but he still could not get inside. Furthermore, the house was in darkness apart from a candle flickering in the window of the maids' attic bedroom.

Finally, he went to the police with his concerns.

One of the policemen who returned to the house with Monsieur Lancelin climbed the wall at the back of the house and gained entry through the kitchen door.

As he cautiously made his way through the house, his path lit only by his flashlight, the policeman could see no signs of a struggle. Everything was in place, giving no clues as to what had happened.

But as he climbed the stairs to the second floor, the beam of light fell on an object on the floor. Small, and round. At first, the policeman couldn't tell what it was, but as he looked closer, he realized to his horror that it was an eyeball.

It became clear to the policeman that more horrors were to come, and he called down to Monsieur Lancelin not to come any further into the house.

As he continued to climb the stairs, the officer stumbled upon the bodies of Madame and Genevieve Lancelin. Or rather, he assumed it was them, as their faces had been smashed with such ferocity that they were unrecognizable. Both women had had their eyes removed, and Madame Lancelin's eyeballs were discovered in the folds of the scarf she was wearing.

The officers were aware that in addition to the Lancelins, there were two maids living in the house. Assuming the bodies they had just discovered had been slaughtered by a madman, they climbed the second flight of stairs to the attic, fearing that they would also find the mutilated bodies of Christine and Léa. They were also mindful of the fact that the murderer, or murderers, might still be in the house.

The door to the maids' room was locked from the inside, and the gendarme could see candlelight flickering from within. Calls to the girls to open the door were futile, so the officers broke down the door, and entered the small attic room.

Christine and Léa Papin were huddled up in bed together, having carefully removed their blood stained clothes and washed their bodies, before putting on clean bedclothes and climbing into bed together.

Next to the bed was a blood soaked hammer.[15]

What Happened Next

The sisters were taken for questioning. Christine was unapologetic in her admission of guilt, explaining matter-of-factly what had happened when the Lancelin women had returned home. Describing the moment that Madame Lancelin lost her temper over the iron, Christine continued:

"Then I rushed down to the kitchen and went to fetch a hammer and a knife, and with both instruments my sister and I fought on our two mistresses, we stabbed [their] heads with a knife, Struck with a pot of tin which was placed on a small table on the landing. We changed the instruments several times from one to the other, that is to say, that I passed to my sister the Hammer to strike and she passed the knife to us, we did the same with the tin pot, and the victims screamed, but I do not remember that they spoke a few words. I went to lock the door and closed the door of the vestibule as well. I closed these doors because I liked it better than the police who noticed our crime before our boss. Then my sister and I went to wash our hands...because we had them full of blood, then we got into our room, we took off our belongings which were stained with blood, we put on a bathrobe, we closed the door to our room, and we went to bed Both in the same bed. This is where you found us when you broke the door. I do not have any regrets or, in other words, I cannot tell you if I do not have any, I prefer to have the skin of my bosses rather than that they have mine or that of my sister. I did not premeditate my crime, I had no hatred towards them, but I do not accept the gesture that Madame Lancelin had for me this evening."

Léa refused to give any account of the evening's events, only to say that she agreed with everything Christine had said, adding:

"Everything [my] sister told you is accurate, the crimes happened exactly as she told you. My role in this case is absolutely the one she told you. I struck as much as she did, and I assert that we had not premeditated to kill our patrons, the idea came to us instantly when we heard that

Madame Lancelin reproached us. [Like] my sister I have no regret for the criminal act we have committed...like my sister, I prefer to have the skin of my bosses rather than those who have had our own."[16]

The Trial

The Papin sisters were brought to trial in September 1933. It was an event which was followed by people all over France, and police had to be drafted in to help control the crowds.

In the run-up to the trial, Christine's behavior became more and more disturbing. The sisters had been separated after their arrest, and Christine displayed sexually driven behavior, calling out for her sister and writhing around on the floor in a sexual manner. She also began to experience the same hallucinations she had while she was with the Lancelins, and on one occasion attempted to gouge her own eyes out, resulting in her being restrained in a straight jacket.

Following this incident, Christine recanted her statement, claiming responsibility for both murders, and saying that Léa had had nothing to do with either of them. Léa, however, continued to take responsibility for her part, and Christine's attempts to free her sister were dismissed at the trial.

The sisters were both found guilty of murder. Christine was sentenced to death by guillotine, while Léa, who had only been charged with the murder of Madame Lancelin, received a lighter sentence of ten years' hard labor, as the jury believed that she had been heavily influenced by her older sister.

Christine's sentence was later commuted to life imprisonment, but she did not fare well. Pining for her beloved Léa, Christine became deeply depressed and stopped eating. She was transferred to an asylum in Rennes, but her condition never improved and she died in 1937 of *cachexia* – literally wasting away.

Léa, on the other hand, fared much better. She kept her head down and did what was asked of her, and after eight years she was released on good behavior. Extraordinarily, she settled in Nantes with her mother,

Clémence, where she assumed the name of Marie and gained employment as a chambermaid.[17]

Léa

In September 1966, an article ran in the newspaper *France-Soir*. A journalist had tracked Léa down and interviewed her. Although the article was factually incorrect, and somewhat moralizing, it gave readers a glimpse into the madness that had taken hold of the youngest Papin sister.

"I do what I can to keep my room simple so that my sister, who watches me from above (because I'm certain she is in Paradise), doesn't laugh at me. I pray for her. I pray for our mother who lived with me until she died. To help me, she said...and all at once I didn't pray anymore. Christine watches me. She is always beautiful and young. She smiles as in the old days: with irony! I come apart, I shrivel up, I sweat from fear, I faint...And there's a trunk in my room."

She talked about her work at the hotel, and the fear she felt every time she made a mistake - of the young chambermaids who worked with her, and the teasing they bestowed upon her.

But her last words to the journalist showed her lack of grasp on reality and the sad delusion she had created for herself.

"When I don't have to work anymore, I want to become Sister Marie, at Bon Pasteur, in Le Mans. I've been saving for it. At Bon Pasteur, one of my older sisters is a nun. I'll go back to her..."[18]

HUSBAND KILLER JANE DOROTIK

ANNA MICHAELS

Murder at the Charisma Ranch

Robert Dorotik was born in 1945, two years before his future wife Jane Marguerite Colvey. It would be 23 years before they would meet and fall in love. They married on April 4, 1970 in Los Angeles California.

Two years later Nicholas was born, another son Alexander would follow shortly after that and by January 16, 1976 their family would be complete with the birth of their daughter Claire Elizabeth.

Robert was an Engineer and Jane was a Health care professional as well as a successful business woman. She made a six figure salary from her 9-5 job alone, and the horse ranch she ran with her daughter was starting to bring in money too.

Robert and Jane would have more than one argument over the money Jane and their daughter Claire spent on Charisma Ranch. He quit his job as an engineer to support Jane's endeavor of raising and training horses. Bob started a business making horse jumps, but by 2000 his business was in trouble. One of the last arguments Jane and Bob had was when Jane and Claire told him they found another horse that would be perfect for the ranch. Robert complained they didn't need any more horses. This infuriated Jane and she told him in no uncertain terms that it was her money and she would spend it how she wanted, she didn't need his permission.

On the afternoon of February 13, 2000 Jane got ready to go down to tend to the horses. Bob was dressing in his jogging clothes and told Jane he was going to go for a run. Bob had been a long distance runner for years. Jane had an injury that prevented her from participating. Jane asked her husband to stoke the fire before he left and she went to the barn.

Mrs. Dorotik returned to the house a couple hours later and Bob was nowhere to be found. She waited a while longer and began looking for him. There were others including neighbors and sons Nick and Alex. Becoming increasingly worried about her husband Jane called the police and told them that he had not come home after his run. A search was organized by the police and in the early morning hours of February 14, 2000 Police found Robert's battered, bloodied body by the side of the road about three miles from home. Police immediately suspected Jane.

Robert Dorotik had died from blunt force trauma and strangulation. He had several injuries to the face and the back of the head (an expert testified the wounds were consistent with a hammer). There were defensive wounds on his hands. He was still wearing his jogging clothes although according to the detectives his shoes were tied in an odd manner. The rope used to strangle him was still around his neck and had made a laceration on his throat.

They did not find blood at the scene that would have been consistent with it being the murder site. Robert had been killed somewhere else and moved here. They found the tire tracks and shoe prints. Jane could not be linked to any of the shoe prints, only the tire tracks. However, hers were not the only tire tracks there, the others were not linked to anyone.

The evidence from the beginning seemed to point at Jane Dorotik as the killer. At the scene where they found the body there were tire tracks that matched the three different treads on her truck. At the residence there was a massive amount of blood that had been cleaned at. Jane claims that the blood was from a nosebleed Robert had and cleaned up. Between the box springs and mattress there was a towel soaked with blood. In a bag in the master bedroom they found a syringe with a horse tranquilizer in it and Jane's fingerprint in Bob's blood was found on it. She was arrested before the blood analysis could even be returned.

Around the room investigators found impact blood spatter patterns as well as drip, transfer and cast off. In one of the closets in the house they found a steam carpet shampooer and a significant amount of cleaning supplies. Bob's blood was found on the cap, handle and nozzle of one of the bottles.

Blood stains consistent with Robert's were found in the bed of the truck Jane, Claire and the ranch hands used around the ranch. They found no blood spatter on his shoes or shirt, but did find some blood on his boxers. One of the two hands never showed up for work the day after Bob's death.

Jane was booked into San Diego County Jail and with the help of family made bail.

Jane's daughter Claire was incriminated in the murder, that she was actually the one that killed Robert, her own father. It was well known that father and daughter had a stormy relationship, and at times became volatile. It was never revealed why the two seemed to hate each other, but Claire even wrote a scathing letter to her father about a "betrayal of trust."

Jane's defense team Kerry Steigerwalt and Cole Casey now had to figure out how to defend their 55 year old client. What they decided on wasn't the most unusual way to do it and it and many other attorneys had done in numerous courtrooms around the country. They deliberately brought Claire up as a suspect. By showing that another person 'could' have committed the murder there is a chance that it will raise enough of a doubt in a jury's mind for them to bring back an acquittal instead of a guilty verdict. This is what the attorney's for Jane were doing, trying to raise a reasonable doubt. This strategy would ultimately tear the family apart. In a letter written three years after her conviction Jane would call her attorney 'ego driven' and the implicating of her daughter a 'seriously flawed defense strategy.'

Prosecutor Bonnie Howard-Regan was convinced that Jane killed her husband to keep from having to pay him spousal support. It seemed there was an impending divorce on the horizon for Bob and Jane. They had separated in 1997 but talked it out and decided to keep their money separate and got back together.

Their own sons commented that their parents' marriage wasn't the most loving and at times their fights became very heated. But is this a motive for murder? Perhaps not just the fights, maybe it was the fact that if the two divorced Jane would have to pay Robert up to 40% of her annual income. This would be upwards of 50,000 dollars a year. Jane was incensed when a divorce attorney had told her that. That is a huge motive for murder in the eyes of the law. There was also a $250,000 life insurance policy on both Bob and Jane. She was forthcoming with the detectives about this during the investigation. If she had to pay that much out in spousal support she wouldn't be able to keep the horse ranch, and it seemed that was all she cared about.

Jane's trial would begin in May of 2001 a little over a year after her husband was murdered. Jane had pled not guilty and was making passionate pleas to the public declaring her innocence. Though her daughter and sister also claimed that Jane was innocent of this heinous crime, Claire, Bonnie Long and a ranch hand all invoked their Fifth Amendment right against self-incrimination. Steigerwalt brought up the fact that Claire's alibi was never confirmed. Had the Sheriff's Department zeroed in on Jane in a hasty attempt to close the case?

On June 9, 2001 the case of Jane Dorotik v The State of California went to the jury for deliberation. After the third day both the defense and the prosecution were starting to worry. Maybe they hadn't presented their case as well as they'd thought. Maybe they didn't explain things in an easy to understand way. In the end however, it wasn't that the jury had a problem understanding what they saw and heard during the trial. They were just being diligent, making sure every juror understood what the evidence was and how it fit in the scheme of things. In fact, they had a unanimous decision on the first vote...guilty on the charge of first degree murder.

Judge Joan Weber said that there was "an overwhelming amount of circumstantial evidence" and when Jane's attorney filed for a new trial it was denied. New witnesses had come forward and Steigerwalt asked that the case be reopened to the jury could hear what they had to say. She denied his request. Weber also asked, "How could you have your husband's blood on your hands if you had nothing to do with his death?" The Judge Weber was referring to the syringe with Janes fingerprint on it. It was an integral piece of evidence in the case.

Without a new trial in San Diego County, the next step is Court Of Appeal Of California, Fourth Appellate District, Division One.

The Court of Appeals works differently than the Trial Court. It is not a place for a new trial or a retrial. They won't look at new evidence or hear from new witnesses. It is strictly for trying to overturn the lower court's decision. If this happens then the Trial Court would be made to do one of several different actions in the case. One would be a whole new trial, which in Jane's case is what her attorney would want to happen. Or perhaps the Appellate Court would order Trial Court to look at additional evidence and/or revisit the facts in the case.

Either of these would be a win for Jane and her defense team. However, before these could happen her attorney would have to show that there was an error in the trial procedure or in how Weber interpreted the law.

This all starts with a Notice to Appeal, and then a brief has to be filed. In many cases appeals are decided based solely on this brief. Other times there will oral arguments before anything is decided.

Janes appeal was filed on November 18, 2003. She is asserting that Judge Weber should have included in the instructions to the jury the lessor charge of voluntary manslaughter because the state didn't present evidence that there was premeditation and aforethought to constitute first degree murder. She was denied.

On June 12, 2009 Jane filed another appeal. There were three key facts in this appeal. In the first one she claims 'ineffective assistance of counsel'. Jane claimed that her defense team didn't represent her properly. They didn't do any investigation of their own.

Second, she believed that not letting the jury hear from the new witnesses and not doing DNA testing jeopardized her case. The rope used to strangle Robert was never test for DNA, claiming that epithelia's of the real killer would have been found.

Third, there were procedural mistakes because of the delayed discovery and her actual innocence.

The defense was not allowed to present evidence that the State's expert witness had many mistakes in other cases by using 'faulty methodology'. The jury was not allowed to hear from an eyewitness.

The Appellate Court denied her, again.

The San Diego Union-Tribune reported on November 22, 2015 that a Judge has determined Jane be allowed to have the DNA in her case tested. The rope used to strangle Bob, the fingernail scrapings, and a piece of hair found around the victim's finger all be tested.

Jane still proclaims her innocence and said the ranch hand that didn't show up for work the day after the murder should be considered. He drives a black pick-up, and his tire tracks were also found at the scene. She also reiterated that the man owed the Dorotik's money.

Jane filed her first appeal on November 18, 2003. The Appellate court upheld the lower court's decision. Then Jane, known also as the petitioner filed Habeas petition on April 4, 2006 in the State Superior Court. Next was a Habeas Petition in the Appellate Court on January 3, 2006. And again Jane filed with the State Supreme Court on November 20, 2006. All appeals and motions to this point had been denied or affirmed the lower court's decision.

On June 1, 2007 Jane would file a Petition for Writ of Habeas Corpus, a Motion to appoint counsel, a Motion for Leave to Proceed in Forma Pauperis and a request for DNA testing. This too was denied or dismissed.

In July of 2007 Jane managed to get the money for filing fees and Magistrate Judge Porter ordered the case be reopened on July 9, 2007.

In the appeal for ineffectual assistance of counsel the superior court "denied the claims on the merits in a written order but only addressed the first two claims. On appeal the Appellate Court did the same thing.

Jane contends that council should have done independent testing of the forensic evidence that the prosecution would be presenting at trial and that there was other available evidence that he could have taken advantage of but didn't. Jane contends that had he done so the findings would have weakened the prosecution's case.

Another point the petitioner brought up is that her counsel didn't call her as a witness in her own defense.

Petitioner wanted a medical professional called as an expert witness to testify as to the medical impossibility that she could have perpetrated the murder due to an injury from an accident years earlier. That she would not have had the strength to do what the prosecution says she did.

Counsel for the defense did not object when a detective testified that he thought she was the killer. He could have also asked for a mistrial also.

He didn't insist on DNA testing prior to the start of the trial, armed with the results of the tests, petitioner is sure that it would have pointed to the real killer or killers.

Petitioner believes that her counsel should have brought up different scenarios that could have explained away the circumstantial evidence brought up at trial.

That he could have provided innocent theories for the incriminating evidence.

He didn't show that police didn't follow any leads, including eyewitnesses that came forward in the early stages of the investigation; they made up their mind that she was guilty. Therefore they didn't look for the real killer/killers.

Jane contends that her counsel could have done their own investigation and found the witnesses that were not heard at trial. Instead he made the leap to blaming Claire Dorotik as a defense.

And finally, follow through on the promises counsel made to the jury about what the evidence would show, and not make a comment to the affect that Jane was guilty.

If none of these ten points were true but the last one, would that fact that her own defense counsel made a comment that directly or indirectly told the jury he thought she was guilty should have been grounds for a mistrial and perhaps proceedings started to disbar her attorney.

The points brought up in Jane's eyes caused her to be wrongly convicted for the murder of her husband.

The forensic evidence in many parts does not support the prosecution's theory. Think about the "blood" found on the wall that supposedly dripped down from the master bedroom upstairs. The man who sold /rented the property to the Dorotik's knew of a water leak. Rain water would get in the track of the sliding door and seep down the wall of the stairs leading to the bedroom. There was Bob's DNA there, but was it from blood? Walking shirtless up the stairs and rubbing his sweaty arm on the wall could leave his DNA, it was not said that it was blood.

Post-conviction reports showed that there was way less blood present than would have been if the State's expert witness, Merrit, were correct. McDonell who did the post-conviction report says the fatal blow probably occurred outside the bedroom. But at the same time doesn't accept the idea that Bob was killed where he was found or that he was killed somewhere else, body dumped where it was found and the blood evidence planted.

McDonell also said that the blood on the mattress could have easily been caused by a bloody nose. That being said it still doesn't explain the different blood stain patterns found throughout the room. Those where found on the pillow, nightstand, walls, bedspread and the window. Those he said cannot be explained away by a nosebleed.

The post-conviction report says that Merrit's testimony was wrong inasmuch as there was not enough blood soaked in to support his idea that Bob remained on the mattress for a long time after the attack.

McDonell concurs with petitioner that the blood around the pot-belly stove could very well have been from the nosebleed. Petitioner wants further testing to find out if it even had anything to do with the murder at all.

The bloody thumb print on the syringe was due to Bob helping Jane with a vet procedure. There was a horse tranquilizer inside the syringe and Jane's thumbprint in Bob's blood on it. This was admitted into evidence? Why, it's said to be a 'key piece' of evidence in the prosecution's case. Petitioner's counsel didn't object? Per Bob's toxicology report there was no drugs in his system. How did they tie it into the murder?

The truck, tire tracks and shoe prints. There was much to do about the tire tracks at the scene where Bob's body was found. There were actually two sets, one belonging to the family truck, the one that everyone including the farm hands had access to. But there was another set, never identified. The shoe prints found also at the scene couldn't be attributed to Jane either. Both sets were too big. The tracks that showed Jane's truck had backed up at the spot where the body was found can easily be explained as well. Bob used the truck to measure jogging routes. If he were to come to the exact length he wanted, he would have just turned around at that spot, hence the backup tracks.

A cursory search of the house was done the evening that Jane reported Bob missing. Police and Police dogs were all in the house including the master bedroom. They didn't find any blood.

Jane was in an accident in 1983 and had a severe injury to a hip which had to be put back together with metal and screws. The prosecution says that Jane would have bludgeoned her husband, then carried him down the stairs from the bedroom, through the house, across a 60' porch and lifted him into the back of a full sized Ford

F250. Defense counsel should have brought up the fact that his client couldn't have done any of that. The Appellate court says that her sons saw her pulling irrigation pipes around the ranch that weighed about 75 lbs. pulling on 75lbs of something is different than lifting 147 lbs of dead weight.

Detective Richard Empson when questioned about the rope used to strangle Robert Dorotik and why it wasn't tested for DNA said the "criminologists in his office discouraged testing it because too many people had handled it." When pressed about the possibility of DNA on it that could have belonged to Claire or the ranch hand Leonel Morales or someone else and lead to the real killer, what then? Empson continued, "I believe I know who killed Bob Dorotik, that's why I arrested Jane Dorotik." Personal opinions are not supposed to be brought in to testimony, especially from an officer of the court. Did Jane's counsel object to this? Did it prejudice the jury against the petitioner? It could be said that it inflamed the jury. Most jurors will believe a law enforcement officer over anyone else. Even if the comment was objected to and stricken from the record the juror's still heard it and no matter if they are told to disregard it, it will still be in their mind.

There are so many points that Jane brought up on each one of her appeals. And each and every one of them were dismissed by the Courts. Many of Jane's friends and family still believe that Jane is innocent and should at least get a new trial so all of the evidence can be heard and that maybe she can even testify in her own defense. Although her trial court attorney believed that doing so was not a good idea. Clearly he didn't believe his client was innocent of the crime.

In the findings of the Appellate Court they say that the petitioner didn't show how not having the jury hear that Merrit's methodology was flawed and that he had been wrong on other cases would not have changed the jury's verdict.

They stated that even though the petitioner believes that the prosecution purposefully did not test for DNA she cannot prove how it would have changed anything. Also added the testing would not have brought forth any exculpatory or impeaching evidence. Knowing that DNA has set wrongfully convicted people free by proving their innocence this statement seems wrong in its entirety. Jane would be in a Catch 22 scenario, she can't prove that by not testing there was an error in law and without being able to prove it would help her case they wouldn't allow the testing.

Jane says she's been through a living hell since being sent to Chowchilla's prison facility in central California. But she hasn't been wasting her time. Along with filing the above mentioned appeals she is fighting for her fellow prisoners who are over the age of 55.

Jane is appalled at how many women are incarcerated and how the number keeps growing every year. She was once a mental health professional and says that a large number of women in prison should be in a Mental Health facility.

According to Jane "Medical care is liken to a third world country." And "there are women dying in prison alone and unnoticed by prison staff.

What she is trying to get done is this, have more compassionate releases, the parole board has the authority to do this but won't. So a program is working its way through legislation in the state of California. "If The Risk Is Low, Let Them Go".

Jane isn't advocating opening the flood gates and letting these women head off to parts unknown. There are a certain set of criteria in place to make sure the risk is actually low.

First of all, they have to have served at least 50% of their sentence or seven years.

They can't have had any disciplinary actions in the past five years. In other words they have to be a model prisoner.

They cannot have any other felony convictions of their record and they must have a concrete, safe place to stay in the community

These are safeguards to keep reoffenders inside the prison walls. Jane is very passionate about this program. She has watched many of what she calls "Golden Girls" languishing with terminal illnesses for years, alone, not able to be with family because Chowchilla houses inmates from all over the state.

Many of the families just don't have the money or time to be able to travel to see their loved ones. And even the children have to be patted down before they can go in to see a relative, to possibly say a last goodbye.

Jane's alternative custody program has to clear through law makers and with the help of different advocates it's headed in the right direction thanks to Carol Lui a senator from California.

This is being heralded as a great program to help with overcrowding of the prisons in California, and if this comes about in a timely manner it could help Jane as well. She is now 68 years old.

HUSBAND KILLER : THE TRUE STORY OF WENDI ANDRIANO

OLIVIA WATSON

Chapter 1

A dying husband needs a devoted wife. But when love runs out, marriage becomes a burden.

On October 8, 2000, Wendi Andriano snapped. She had played the part of devoted wife to her terminally ill husband, Joe Andriano, for years, but when the love left their marriage, so did Wendi's patience for her husband's eventual demise.

Wendi had a plan to help nudge nature along, and when her plan b expired, she took matters directly into her own hands and bludgeoned him to death.

Wendi first tried to poison her husband by spiking his last meal, a homemade beef stew, with sodium azide, but Joe Andriano did not ingest enough to kill him, only enough to vomit it back up. Wendi then grabbed the nearest object, a bar stool, and beat her dying husband over the head so many times that parts of his brain became exposed.

After thinking she had successfully killed her husband twice, Wendi then realized that Joe was still breathing, so she took a knife from the family kitchen and stabbed him in the side of the throat.

Minutes later, Joe was finally dead.

This bizarre and frantic way Wendi killed her husband isn't the strangest thing about the case though. Known even to Wendi, Joe was due to die from terminal cancer within the next few years anyways.

Why Wendi couldn't wait to kill her husband is an intriguing tale wrought with sex, lies, and strangely, a lack of patience.

Chapter 2

Wendi and Joe Andriano grew up together in the small farming community of Casa Grande, Arizona. But while they both had gone to the same school, they never dated. As a minister's daughter, Wendi's social life was restricted to her father's church. Her celebration for graduating high school was even in the form of a missionary trip to Mexico in 1989. When she returned she took a job at the local clerical hospital.

Wendi met Joe in 1992 through friends. Although when the couple started dating Joe's family found the minister's daughter to be an unusual fit for the loud, outgoing former football player, they all thought she was friendly enough and approved of the match.

Joe worked for a local boat builder. He was very mechanically inclined and was a very good welder. He owned his own boat and took Wendi for several cruises around the local hot spots for speedboats. They were inseparable.

The couple married in January of 1994. Their wedding took place in a baptist church across the street from their shared elementary school. Their reception was at the Elk's club and was populated by their many friends and family. Even after two years of dating, though, Joe's family felt like they didn't know his new bride very well, but Joe seemed to be very happy, so they were happy for him.

Soon after marrying, the couple became business partners when they started a small company that did windshield repair and replacement. The business combined Wendi's office experience with Joe's mechanical experience, skills they both exceeded at, and the business thrived.

The couple hadn't been married a whole year yet before they faced their first major challenge together. That fall, Joe noticed an odd bump on his neck. When he had it tested, he was told it was a non-cancerous benign tumor, but it wasn't long before they were second-guessing the diagnoses. A year after it was removed, the tumor grew back.

A second surgery and round of tests seemed to reconfirm that the tumor was benign, but shortly after Wendi gave birth to a son in 1997, the tumor was back yet again.

The third time the tumor returned, Joe's wife and family were convinced that the tumor had to be cancer. This fear was confirmed in 1998 when Joe underwent surgery to have the bump removed for the fourth time. Joe's pre-surgery chest x-ray showed that not only was the tumor cancerous, but that the cancer had now spread across Joe's throat, chest, and lungs.

The prognosis wasn't good—Joe had a rare form of cancer and while radiation and chemotherapy were standard, there was no guarantee they would work. On top of this, Wendi was also pregnant again and was only months away from giving birth to the couple's second child.

Chapter 3

In an effort to increase Joe's chances of survival while decreasing his suffering, Wendi and Joe decided to pursue holistic treatments before resorting to chemotherapy and radiation. They had been told that chemotherapy and radiation treatments would likely not cure Joe, but they would lengthen his life by a few years; however, these years would be anything from pleasant. The horrific side-effects chemotherapy and radiation treatments cause are well known.

So the Andriano's decided first to try anything from special diets to alternative medical treatments to prayer—anything that had a chance to help Joe. Joe even attended a holistic treatment centre for cancer patients in Colorado for a few weeks where he was surrounded by other men and women facing the same prognosis as him. After seeing the bravery of others in the same position as him, Joe began thinking about his future again and began to see it as bright for the first time in a while.

After Joe returned from his holistic healing getaway with a bright new attitude, the Andriano's decided the next best step would be for Joe to begin chemotherapy treatments. He had begun to crave his future and was ready to take steps to achieve it. Unfortunately, taking these steps meant that Joe needed to quit his welding job as well as his own position in the couple's business.

To help make ends meet, Wendi returned to working for the first time since the birth of the couple's children. She ended up taking multiple jobs and worked long hours while continuing to care for her husband at home. Eventually, Wendi landed a job managing the San

Riva apartment complex in the Ahwatukee foothills, an upscale neighbourhood outside of Phoenix.

Wendi's new job came with some major perks—the salary was above average, which was nice as Wendi was now the family's breadwinner, and it required Wendi to live on site, which meant that the family now lived in a luxury apartment but paid no rent. Wendi's new job also gave her a new life. A large part of her duties as complex manager was arranging social activities for the other residents of the San Riva apartments, who were mostly young, wealthy, single businesspeople.

Every Saturday the complex hosted picnics, pool parties, or late-night socials. The residents even had their own baseball team. Wendi was required to attend every event, which meant Joe was needed to stay home with their two children. Wendi enjoyed this alone time so much that many of the residents at the San Riva had no clue she had a dying husband and two children at home. She partied like she was single.

The first few months at the San Riva went well. Wendi organized mixers and pool parties for the tenants while Joe took care of the kids. Despite being very weak from treatments, he did everything he could, he wanted to do it. He prefered to have his kids around him even when he didn't feel good.

Although they had never gotten close to their daughter-in-law, Joe's parents also pitched in with babysitting so the couple could have time alone together. They didn't get to see each other much as Wendi began spending more and more time at work. Her new job had also given her a new confidence, and she spent many nights out on the town dancing and drinking away her weekday stress with friends. Joe began to fear that Wendi would soon leave him for her new lifestyle, but this fear got sidetracked when his health continued to fail.

In the summer of 2000, when tests revealed his cancer had spread yet again, Joe and Wendi decided to increase the frequency of Joe's chemotherapy. Joe agreed to undergo more treatments, but they quickly took their toll. He lost 15 pounds in the first week alone, and Joe's doctor became concerned. It went from bad to worse very quickly.

By the beginning of October 2000, it became harder and harder to remain optimistic about Joe's chances of beating his cancer. It became apparent it was terminal, but doctors insisted that with treatment Joe could live for several more years.

No one had any idea that Joe would be dead after only the first week of the month. No one, that is, except for one person—Wendi Andriano.

Chapter 4

Just after 2:00 a.m. on October 8, Wendi Andriano called a friend who also lived in the San Riva apartment complex. She told her friend that she needed someone to stay with the kids while she took Joe to the hospital. When the friend arrived, she found Joe on the floor, barely alive.

Joe was on the floor in the fetal position. There was vomit on the floor around him and he couldn't stand up. Wendi confided in her friend that she told Joe that she had called 9-1-1 and paramedics were on the way, but this wasn't true. After seeing Joe in such poor condition, the neighbour urged Wendi to call paramedics. She then went outside to wait for them to arrive while Wendi waiting with her husband.

Wendi did call 9-1-1, but when the EMT's arrived minutes later, she refused to let them or her friend inside the apartment. She said that her husband was dying from terminal cancer and had a do not resuscitate order. Joe was not to receive any medical attention.

Just over an hour later, at 3:30 a.m., Wendi dialed 9-1-1 a second time. The same team of paramedics came to the house. It didn't take them long to realize something wasn't quite right, so they contacted the police department. Both the paramedics and the police were shocked to find out that Joe, who had been terminally ill from cancer for quite some time had died, but not from the cancer that had been slowly killing his body. He died from being repeatedly beaten with a bar stool and from being stabbed in the neck.

When the police opened the front door of the apartment, they were confronted with obvious signs of a deadly struggle. The apartment was in a complete state of disarray, and there was blood everywhere. Blood had been traced throughout the kitchen, the dining room, and the living room of the luxury apartment, and blood had spattered across the walls the ceilings. Lying in the middle of the bloody scene was Joe, with a knife wound in his neck and holes spattered across his visible skull.

While crime scene technicians surveyed the apartment, phoenix police took Wendi down to the station for a formal statement. She was wearing clothes drenched in Joe's blood and was armed with a story that explained how Joe's death had been a complete accident.

In the interrogation room, Wendi told police she and joe had spent the evening in Casa Grande visiting with Joe's parents. They put the kids to bed after they returned home, which was when Joe noticed something odd about Wendi's appearance—she wasn't wearing her wedding ring.

According to Wendi, Joe worked himself into a rage and began accusing her of having an affair. This argument turned into a shoving match, and when Joe grabbed a belt, Wendi grabbed a bar stool and swung. Joe went down on all fours so she hit him again. It was then that she called her neighbour for help. Joe may have been in a terrible state when the neighbour saw him, but according to Wendi when she went outside Joe had gotten back to his feet easily.

Wendi said she denied the EMTs access to the apartment because she and Joe were both embarrassed about the fight, but just minutes after the EMTs left, the fight got physical again.

Wendi said that her husband tried to strangle her with a telephone cord and she defended herself with the first weapon she could get in her hands—a kitchen knife. She was vague about how the knife ended up in Joe's neck though, saying she was holding the knife up when Joe suddenly fell flat on his face. The next thing she knew, blood was spurting everywhere. He must have fallen on the blade, it was simply an accident.

Many things about this story didn't make sense to the police. First of all, the timeline presented in Wendi's story didn't match the accounts of Wendi's neighbour or the EMTs. Wendi's neighbour had seen no evidence of a physical fight when they first entered the apartment—there were no broken bar stools or blood like later when the police arrived. As well, Wendi had few injuries on her body, definitely no injuries that would necessitate self defence in the form of murder.

Joe's illness also shed doubt on Wendi's story. Joe's parents told police that when the Andriano's visited earlier that evening, Joe had been so weak from his treatments that he could barely stand. They had spent the evening doting on their sick son, bringing him any comforts he wanted. If he was too weak to stand, he certainly couldn't have been strong enough to violently attack Wendi.

Police also uncovered a damning piece of evidence from Wendi herself, in a moment when she thought she was all alone. The investigators that had been questioning Wendi left her on her own in the interrogation room for some time while they fact checked some of her statements and checked in with the investigators who were scanning the crime scene for evidence. During this time, Wendi made a phone call to a coworker at the apartment complex and asked them to hide some of her files from the police. This immediately led to a search of Wendi's office where police found evidence that Wendi had in fact killed her husband. She had even been planning it for months.

Chapter 5

While both investigators strongly believed that Wendi Andriano was responsible for Joe's death, they were stumped by her motive. Why would Wendi kill her dying husband? The police didn't know, but they did have one intriguing lead—the phone call Wendi had made from the interrogation room. They were determined to find out what she was trying to hide.

When they searched her office, police discovered that Wendi had been disciplined at work for using her computer to search inappropriate items on the internet while on the clock.She had been conducting research on poisons, and how to use certain poisons to kill people. They also discovered the papers that she had tried to hide—shipping notices for a substance known as sodium azide.

Sodium azide is a lethal substance with a variety of industrial uses including propelling airbags. It is not, however, something that the average person can simply go out and buy. It's not restricted to the point where only certain companies can possess it, but it needs to be bought for a reason—something that an apartment complex didn't have. But based on the information on the shipping invoice, Wendi had found a way around that.

Wendi had created a fictitious business license using the tax ID form for the apartment complex. Using a Xerox machine and an exacto knife, Wendi had removed all information specific to the apartment complex and inserted fictitious information for a fake company.

The business name on the shipping notice was bogus, but the address wasn't. Wendi had the substance delivered to an address in Scottsdale, Arizona in an attempt to distance herself, but that plan didn't work. When the police tracked down the real address on the invoice, workers at the company positively identified Wendi as the person who had come by a couple weeks earlier to pick up a package she had mistakenly had shipped there instead of her own office.

Wendi's coworkers had seen her with a package but that she had been very mysterious with the contents. She refused to tell anyone what was inside. Had this been the sodium azide? And if so, where was it now?

Chapter 6

Suspecting that Wendi had tried to poison Joe with the sodium azide, police took samples of every medication and food they could find in the Andriano's apartment. If Joe had ingested poison, it would have explained the awful state Wendi's friend had seen him in just over an hour before he died. Luckily, the remainders of Joe's last supper, homemade beef stew, still sat in a pot on the stove.

However, police didn't find any evidence of Wendi's mysterious package, or any evidence of the sodium azide itself in Wendi and Joe's apartment. They had just begun to lose hope in finding the poison when they found out Wendi had a storage space in the building that she failed to tell the police about. Hidden behind a stack of boxes in Wendi's storage unit was a small bottle of white powder and a measuring spoon. The white powder was soon identified as sodium azide.

But the storage unit wasn't the only place investigators found the lethal substance—it was also in Joe's stomach contents and in the beef stew on the stove.

While discovering the poison helped police understand that Wendi had been trying to kill her husband, it didn't explain why she had bludgeoned him to death on October 8, 2000. Wendi had spent a lot of time researching poisons and she spent a lot of time manufacturing documents so that she could purchase the poison. It certainly wasn't a spur of the moment decision.

But why would Wendi beat and stab her husband if she had already poisoned him? Prosecutors had a theory, one that would cut to the heart of the crime. It was patience—or more precisely, Wendi's lack of it—that had killed Joe in the end.

Wendi had grown tired of waiting for the cancer to kill Joe, so she decided to give nature a little nudge by poisoning his supper. But according to the theory, when Wendi gave Joe the poison, things didn't go quite to plan. Joe hadn't ingested enough poison to kill him when he began vomiting it back up. With her plan quickly failing, Wendi panicked. She snapped.

Now improvising, Wendi beat Joe with the nearest object she could get her hands on—a bar stool. Pathologists were able to conclude that Wendi beat Joe over the head with the stool no less than twenty-four times. This beating did render Joe unconscious, but still didn't kill him so Wendi grabbed a kitchen knife and stabbed him in the part of his body that caused all this trouble in the first place—the side of his neck.

Chapter 7

Ten days after she murdered her husband, Wendi Andriano was formally charged with first degree murder. Wendi's crime was viewed as being especially cruel due to the large amount of suffering Joe had had to endure over several hours thanks to Wendi's actions. Because of this, the prosecutor's on Wendi's trial did the almost unthinkable, they sought the death penalty.

When Wendi a walked into the Arizona courtroom on September 9, 2004 she looked vastly different from the perky apartment manager that the residents of the San Riva apartments used to know.

At the time of the killing she had been blonde, she had short hair, and generally appeared to be much younger and cute than the individual who appeared in court with long dark hair and thick glasses. Previously, she had liked to look good and show her figure so her conservative dress at the trial was certainly different from the look her friends were used to seeing. She was trying to look more conservative, more innocent.

She had had plenty of time to perfect her new look—it had taken prosecutors almost four years to bring the case to trial. It had been postponed about 12 times before it was finally brought before a judge and jury.

In their opening statement, prosecutors reminded the jury that at the time of the murder Wendi had been anything but the perfect mother or wife she claimed to have been. She had been someone who had no disregard for her husband at all. While her husband was dying, she had gone out partying and started affairs, and when his condition worsened, and it began to cramp her style, she turned to poison.

Wendi didn't like her new role as family breadwinner, especially with the loss of Joe's income, and with rising medical bills, the family was in the worst financial state they had ever been in. Wendi had thought she was going to be able to be a stay-at-home-mom for the rest of her life, and she did not adjust well to her return to the workforce. So Wendi had found an out.

Although Joe did not have any life insurance, even though Wendi had asked several friends to pretend to be Joe in medical exams so he could be insured, Joe had filed a malpractice suit against his former doctor who had continually told him his tumor was benign when it was in fact spreading throughout his body. If Joe died and the lawsuit went through, Wendi would likely walk away with a multi-million dollar settlement.

More than money though, Wendi had wanted freedom. She wanted the freedom to be single again, she wanted freedom to the ball-and-chain who was slowly dragging her spirit into his grave along with himself. Wendi wanted to not have to care about her dying husband anymore, who was too weak to provide her with any love.

Wendi maintained her plea of innocence throughout the trial, and her defence team attempted to prove she had been the victim of abuse not only on the night of Joe's death but also throughout the couple's entire marriage. To explain the poison, Wendi told the court that Joe had been the one who had grown tired of waiting for the cancer to end his life, and had asked Wendi to help him do it himself.

On the witness stand Wendi said that Joe had willingly taken the poison, but she also stuck by the story that she had originally told police, that Joe had suspected an affair and became enraged when she affirmed them. He became deranged and attacked her, starting the bloody fight. Wendi claimed Joe had died during the ensuing struggle.

Wendi's story wasn't enough to convince the court though, and on November 18, 2004 she was found guilty of the crime. It had taken the jury only two-and-a-half-hours to come to its unanimous decision. Six years after her husband joe had been diagnosed with terminal cancer, Wendi Andriano faced a possible death sentence of her own.

On December 20, 2004, the jurors assigned to Wendi Andriano's case met and decided on Wendi's fate—it would be death for Ms Andriano. Wendi, along with most of the courtroom, was aghast. Even Joe's family was shocked by the decision. Wendi Andriano became the second ever woman to be put on death row in Arizona, a state that reserves the death penalty for the worst of the worst.

Wendi Andriano has since attempted to appeal the court's decision, but as of early 2017, all attempts have been denied and Wendi continues to wait on death row. Wendi and Joe's children now live with Joe's parents, who continue to mourn the loss of their beloved son.

Joe Andriano's death was especially long, and especially cruel, but no happy ending was found when Wendi was sentenced to her own death. Many view the conclusion of this case to be the saddest possible outcome. On October 8, 2000, two lives were lost, and two children were left without parents.

THE SUNSET STRIP KILLER: The True Story of Carol Bundy

Jessi Gaines

Born Carol Mary Peters on August, 26, 1942, Carol Bundy's childhood, much like her adulthood, was spent pursuing a desperate need for attention and validation. Bundy's ability to idealize or overlook any unpleasantness made her a perfect victim for manipulators and abusers looking for a potential victim – a talent she picked up early on to deal with the abuses of her parents, Charles and Gladys Peters.

Bundy's memories of her childhood are happy ones – Christmases where her parents refused to let their three children miss out on the special holiday because of a lack of money, or her father's attempt to convince her that the tooth fairy had visited overnight, using a doll's feet to leave footprints through Bundy's bedroom. Bundy's mother worked as a hairdresser, but had previously been a stand-in for tap-dancer Ruby Keeler – and Bundy remembered her as a woman who exuded beauty and glamour.

Bundy, on the other hand, was awkward and unattractive, leading her mother to begin treating her as though she didn't even exist. When she was eight, Bundy came home to a locked door, and no matter how much she cried or begged her mother to let her in, Gladys refused – stating that Bundy was not her daughter. Eventually, Charles persuaded Gladys to let the girl in, but even though Bundy was allowed back into the home, her mother ignored her completely.

However, Charles was not without reproach. Gladys, who had a tendency to beat the children relentlessly with a belt, wasn't permitted to hit Bundy or her siblings – but Charles was fond of using physical abuse to assert his dominance. While Bundy remembers her father's beatings as fitting to the severity of the offense, Charles was an alcoholic who used Gladys' death as an excuse to move his assaults on his daughters from physical to sexual.

For eight months, Charles molested both Bundy and her sister Vicky, telling the girls it was their responsibility to "take their mother's place in his bed." Although Vicky maintains that the sexual abuse continued until Charles remarried, Bundy can only recall one instance where her father molested her – and described him as a good man, who loved her.

When Charles remarried, though, he began abusing Bundy more often – beating her, degrading her, humiliating her. He told her she was stupid and fat, and even that he wanted to kill her and the rest of the family – but he'd only gotten as far as the cat before his new wife had taken away his gun. After staying in foster homes, with their grandmother, and with an uncle, the girls were brought back to live with their father in California.

Desperate measures

At this point, Bundy was willing to do anything to get away from her father – and at the age of 17, she married a 56-year-old alcoholic to try and escape the abuse. Bundy had discovered how to use her sexuality and large breasts to seduce men and receive the attention she so desperately needed – but she was unwilling to prostitute herself for her new husband. When she left him, Bundy took up with another older man, a 32-year-old writer named Richard Geis.

With encouragement from Geis, who appreciated her wit and intelligence, Bundy embarked on a brief but somewhat successful writing career. However, after her father hung himself in 1962, Bundy sought comfort through sexual encounters with women. Bouncing frequently between male lovers and female lovers, Bundy was unable to find a reliable source of the attention she needed, so she eventually returned to Geis and the couple moved to Oregon.

Still, Bundy would occasionally let other men pay her for sex. Instead of urging her to seek counseling, Geis agreed to support Bundy while she attended nursing school in Santa Monica – he would pay for her education as long as she kept her grades up. In fact, Bundy was named class valedictorian when she completed the program in 1968.

It was in nursing school that Bundy met her next husband, Grant. Their relationship started off well, and continued to be relatively stable until the birth of their first son – but then, Bundy claimed, he started beating and belittling her. By the time Bundy had given birth to their second son, her eyesight had deteriorated to the point where it looked like she may have to give up nursing. Grant was faced with the prospect of being saddled with the responsibility of caring for a blind wife, as well as their two children, and grew increasingly more violent.

Bundy escaped the abusive marriage and took her two boys to a womens' shelter in 1979, where she stayed for two weeks before finding a small apartment in Van Nuys. The managers of the Valerio Gardens apartment building, Jeanette and John "Jack" Murray, took pity on the poor single mother, and Jack was frequently called on to help Bundy with issues at the apartment. Despite her husband's established pattern of cheating, Jeanette wasn't concerned about the 36-year-old month – Bundy was overweight with short brown hair, a stark contrast to Murray's typical blonde, long-legged mistresses.

The object of her affection

The kindness she saw from Murray led Bundy to develop a crush on her landlord, who took her to the Social Security office so she could receive disability payments and even to the optometrist, to get her fitted for a pair of glasses to help the single mother return to work. Murray, for his part, enjoyed having a captive audience. Good looking, with a fantastic voice, Murray had come to America from Australia to pursue a career in music – but had been unable to make it as a performer thanks to his arrogant attitude.

The two found exactly what they needed in each other, and soon began a sexual relationship. Bundy's crush rapidly became an obsession, and she started coming up with more frequent excuses to have her landlord visit her property. Her infatuation for Murray convinced Bundy that he was in love with her, too – even though he told her it would be years before he would be able to leave his wife. Bundy was well-versed in the art of overlooking negative or painful thoughts and feelings, and continued to look for ways to strengthen the connection she saw with Murray.

Regularly, Bundy loaned her landlord money and bought him expensive gifts after she received the settlement from the sale of the house she'd owned with Grant. She also opened a joint safety deposit box with Murray, and made deposits to help him cover the expenses he said he was incurring as a result of his wife's alleged cancer treatments. Still, Murray wasn't giving Bundy the attention she craved, and she started up a brief affair with Jeanette's younger brother.

In an attempt to spend some time alone with her lover, Bundy arranged a weekend for her and Murray in Las Vegas – as a "reward" for all of his help, she said. However, after the couple checked in at the hotel and took in a show, Murray left Bundy alone for the remainder of the weekend while he gambled. He returned in time to fly back with Bundy, and, hurt and upset, Bundy forgot her suitcase in Murray's van.

When Jeanette showed up at Bundy's door with the forgotten suitcase, Bundy used the opportunity to try and bring her affair with Murray to his wife's attention – thinking Murray would then be forced to leave his wife and finally be with Bundy. During their discussion, Bundy learned that Jeanette never had cancer, and she immediately confronted Murray. While Bundy was initially angry to learn that the money she'd given him to pay for the treatments had actually been used to pay off Murray's van, he calmed her down by reassuring her that his intention was still to leave his wife and eventually be with Bundy. Eventually.

However, Bundy was losing her patience. On Christmas Day, when Murray didn't show up to spend any time with her and her children, she made the decision to take matters into her own hands. Bundy attempted to bribe Jeanette into leaving her husband – which Jeanette accepted, as long as this was Murray's desire, as well. Bundy left with the hope that later that evening, she and Murray would finally be able to start their life together. But when Murray came to talk to her after discussing the situation with his wife, he told Bundy to "stay out of his life," telling her there was "no way" he would let her break up his family.

Devastated, Bundy spent a few days licking her wounds, but still turned up three days later at Murray's favorite bar, the "Little Nashville Club." Murray regularly played music at the bar, but that night, he was simply enjoying himself off-stage, dancing with his wife. Heartbroken, Bundy felt her dream of a life with Murray slip further and further away – but caught the eye of an attractive blond gentleman, who she saw watching her from across the bar.

After an evening of dancing, Bundy was taken with the stranger from the bar. Rather than taking advantage of her promiscuity, this new man treated Bundy with respect – which made her feel like a true lady, cherished and appreciated. Charmed, Bundy felt like she and Doug Clark were made for each other, and was already looking forward to seeing him again when he dropped her off at home and promised to call on her soon.

A whirlwind romance

Doug Clark waited only a few days before calling Bundy and asking to see her again. Although Bundy preferred to keep her male callers away from her children, she relented when Clark suggested he come over for dinner – and was pleased to see that her boys took to him immediately. They played, cuddled, and Clark even tucked the boys in for bed before telling them that he would be spending the night with their mother. Bundy loved the way he took care of things, and was more than willing to give him complete control.

For the first time, Bundy made love with a partner who seemed truly interested in giving her pleasure, rather than just letting her do all the work. He was an affectionate lover, telling her over and over again how much he wanted her, how much he appreciated her, how smart and beautiful she was. This was all new to Bundy, and played right into her desperate need for validation.

The next morning, however, Bundy awoke to see Clark looking concerned and anxious – his landlady was causing him grief, he said, so would she mind terribly if he moved some of his things into her apartment? Enamoured, Bundy was eager to accommodate Clark's desires, even when he requested a pair of her panties – just so he could remember her, even when they were apart. Although she felt somewhat uncomfortable with it, Bundy gave her new lover a pair of her large, cotton panties, which he promptly returned to her when he saw how big they were. Bundy was hurt, but she was still thrilled to have found such an attractive, caring, respectful man who was so interested in her.

Still, Clark's attentions weren't enough to tear Bundy away from Murray. After sending him several letters professing her deep, unwavering love for him, Bundy made another attempt to manipulate him away from his wife. This time, though, Murray refused to indulge Bundy's long-standing delusions, and told her it was finally time to move out of the building. Although reluctant, Bundy moved into a new apartment just three miles away – big enough for herself, her two sons, and her new lover.

After moving her furniture into the new suite, Murray left with his wife, but returned frequently to have sex with Bundy or persuade her into lending him more money. Not surprisingly, Murray and Clark disliked each other immediately, which Bundy interpreted as jealousy – a sign of their love for her. She told Clark how Murray had exploited her affection for him by asking for loans and gifts. Enraged, Clark demanded that Bundy cut him off immediately. She agreed, but kept the joint account open.

The perfect couple

Clark's anger over Murray's mistreatment of Bundy encouraged her enough to overlook the fact that her new live-in boyfriend wasn't covering his share of the rent, bills, or food. Bundy's new job at Valley Medical Centre, where she was now working as a vocational nurse, paid her more than enough to cover the expenses – and Bundy was content to take care of everything, as long as Clark continued to provide her with his love and affection.

Unfortunately, Clark was having a hard time keeping this up. He was proving himself to be just as self-absorbed as Murray – talking constantly about himself and his needs, with no real interest in hearing about anything Bundy brought up. However, the couple grew closer together after Clark read an article about expressing true love by fulfilling each other's fantasies. Eagerly, Clark convinced Bundy to start opening up about her own sexual desires, and he began to do the same.

Clark's fantasies were dark, but Bundy was thrilled that he was sharing these intimate thoughts with her. Bundy had a budding interest in bondage and domination, and particularly enjoyed imagining herself as Clark's captured sex slave – although in his fantasy, this role was filled by some young girl. But Clark loved that Bundy's sexual limits seemed virtually non-existent, and he pushed to include even darker subject matter, even murder. If she loved him, Clark told Bundy, she "should be willing to kill for him." Desperate to please him, she assured him that she would.

Their relationship was inconsistent. Clark would regularly disappear for hours and even days at a time, withdrawing from Bundy and drawing out her deepest insecurities. When he would eventually return, Bundy would be so relieved and happy to see him that she would say anything to convince him to stay. She also continued to react with pleasure and excitement as Clark's nighttime fantasy sharing grew increasingly sordid and graphic – even when he told her details of an ex-girlfriend's experiences with necrophilia.

A near escape

Bundy's penchant for promiscuity led her to browse personal ads occasionally, especially during Clark's frequent absences. When a posting from a well-to-do studio executive named Art Pollinger caught her eye, Bundy bravely responded to the ad. Pollinger weighed nearly four hundred pounds, but he was looking for a wife and thought Bundy a worthy prospect. Her tried-and-true method of using her past abuses to entice new lovers paid off again, and Pollinger – who genuinely enjoyed Bundy's company and thought her to be an intelligent and interesting woman – encouraged her to cut ties with Murray.

Eventually, after some persuading, Bundy allowed Polliger to drive her to the bank, where she withdrew the money she had left in the joint safety-deposit box she'd opened with Murray. Nearly $6000 was missing, and withdrawal slips were signed with Murray's name, but Bundy continued to defend Murray's deceit. Still, she took the rest of the money and put it in a chequing account where Murray would be unable to access it.

Despite Pollinger's genuine affection and desire to share his life with Bundy, the two ended up parting ways. Bundy was used to the emotional abuse she had endured in her previous relationships, and couldn't be satisfied in a healthy relationship.

Red flags

After having surgery to restore her sight, Bundy was excited at the prospect of purchasing a new car – and so was Clark, who had selected a blue 1973 Buick station wagon. Even though the car was large and difficult for Bundy to drive, since her peripheral vision was severely limited, she bought it anyway. She was desperate to give Clark everything he asked for – even guns, which he said she should have for protection. From a pawn shop in Van Nuys, Clark selected two .25 calibre Raven automatics, which Bundy was more than willing to pay for and register in her own name.

By now, Bundy's older son was starting to notice how Clark dominated his mother, and begged her to kick him out. Instead of taking her child's concern to heart, however, Bundy refused to acknowledge Clark's abuse – choosing to lash out at her son, instead. Clark and Bundy regularly beat him, and once, Clark even graphically detailed how he could kill the boy – with Bundy's son right next to him. Rather than defending her child, though, Bundy merely watched as Clark's behaviour grew more and more violent.

The couple had even stopped having sex, as Clark informed Bundy that she was too unattractive to arouse him anymore. Desperate to please him, Bundy began accompanying Clark as he picked up prostitutes from the Sunset Strip, and would watch from the backseat while he forced the usually young women to service him orally.

According to former FBI Special Agent Robert R. Hazelwood, who worked with the Behavioural Sciences Unit, men like Clark employ a specific process that can turn vulnerable women into accomplices. After identifying a woman like Bundy, desperate for attention, they use seduction techniques to reshape the woman's sexual norms – even if the woman is initially disturbed or frightened.

"These men have the ability to recognize vulnerable women and manipulate them," Hazelwood said. "The behaviour gets reinforced with attention and affection, gifts and excitement. Eventually, they are doing things that isolate them and further lower their self-esteem. All they have is this guy, so they cooperate."

Clark had plenty of experience in charming women enough to get them to do whatever he wanted, but although he had tried, he had been unable to find a suitable woman to replace Bundy. None of the other women he dated were as willing to indulge his dark sexual fantasies as Bundy was, so despite his mounting contempt for her, Clark continued to live with Bundy on and off. Bundy reassured herself that even though Clark had other girlfriends, she was the one he shared his intimate fantasies with – his feelings for her, she thought, must be deeper.

More than just fantasies

When Clark showed up at her apartment in late April, 1980, covered in blood, Bundy realized his murderous tendencies had taken a step beyond his imagination. Although Bundy chose to believe a fabricated tale Clark wove where he'd been attacked by a girl's boyfriend, the real story came out when a young prostitute named Charlene identified Doug Clark as the man who had stabbed her repeatedly with a knife after picking her up and requesting oral sex. She had been lucky to escape alive.

Bundy's suspicions mounted further when she discovered a bag of clothes and a blanket in the backseat of the Buick – covered in blood. When she confronted Clark, he told her the same kind of graphic story of sexual perversion that she'd become accustomed to hearing – only this time, the story was real.

Clark had spotted two young runaways, 15-year-old Cindy and her 16-year-old stepsister, Gina, at a bus stop. After picking them up and demanding Cindy give him oral sex, he told Bundy that he shot both girls until they were dead and then drove with the bodies to a garage he rented in Burbank. Once inside the garage, Clark said he dragged the bodies onto an old mattress and proceeded to perform acts of necrophilia on their corpses.

That night, after confessing to Bundy, Clark returned to the garage with a camera borrowed from one of his other girlfriends. After playing with the bodies again, he wrapped them in the blanket and dumped them in a ditch off the Ventura Freeway. Bundy was thrilled that he'd chosen to confess this activity to her, instead of any of the other women he was involved with.

Still, Bundy felt compelled to report the murders to the Van Nuys police. When she called the department the night after Clark's confession, she told the officer that she believed her boyfriend had committed the crime. Although Bundy told the officer some details of the case, she wasn't taken seriously, and when the call was disconnected, they assumed the "crank caller" had just hung up.

Clark started telling Bundy about other murders he claimed to have committed, including the killing of a man named Vic Weiss and the slaying of a young prostitute identified by police as teenage runaway Marnett Comer. Their relationship had become completely centered around Clark's murderous desires and Bundy's desperate need for his attention. Even though he no longer made any attempt to flatter or even be kind to Bundy, Clark had her completely under his control.

Only a few months later, at the end of June, Bundy accompanied Clark on what would be their first murder together. Cathy, who the couple picked up off Hollywood's Highland Avenue, looked about 17 years old, and agreed to perform oral sex on Clark for $30. Bundy, watching from the backseat, passed Clark the gun when Cathy failed to get him erect. He shot her, and as she lay dying with her head in Bundy's lap, Clark drove the car out into the country. Cathy was left along a gravel road near the Magic Mountain amusement park.

The very next night, Clark came home and told Bundy of another killing. He'd spotted three prostitutes working together, and convinced one of them, Exxie Wilson, to get in the Buick. After killing her and cutting off her head, Clark realized the other two women might be able to identify him if Wilson's body was found, so he went back and picked up one of the other prostitutes, later identified as Karen Jones. Clark left Jones' body near the Burbank Studios, and, after giving up on finding the third girl, returned to Bundy's apartment with Wilson's head.

They kept the head in the freezer for a few days, and Clark told Bundy how he would take it into the shower with him and push his penis into the open mouth. Eventually, Bundy cleaned the head and put it in an ornate treasure chest, which they dumped near the Studio City Sizzler where Clark had left the rest of Wilson's body. The chest was discovered almost immediately, and the relationship between Bundy and Clark grew even more strained.

The unraveling

In an attempt to gain back Clark's affections, Bundy agreed to participate in a three-way sexual relationship involving their 11-year-old neighbour, who Clark had been molesting for months. Since news of the Sunset Strip murders was spreading, prostitutes were hesitant to work alone, and it was increasingly difficult for Clark and Bundy to find anyone willing to get in their car.

Police were holding press conferences where they discussed evidence that seemed to link the cases – leading them to believe this may be the work of a serial killer. It was even suspected that the killer lived in the area, Detective Sergeant John Helvin stated to the press, "but we don't know for sure."

The stress of this ongoing investigation and Clark's lack of interest in her led Bundy to a desperate suicide attempt, and when she woke up alone at a hospital in Burbank, Bundy called Murray to come pick her up.

Bundy was willing to do anything to reignite Murray's sexual interest in her, so she started bringing her young neighbour for him to fondle. When that still wasn't enough, Bundy turned to her reliable method of playing the victim to gain her lover's sympathy – she told Murray about the murders. Although Murray didn't threaten to tell the police, Bundy knew she couldn't keep him alive. Besides, this was her opportunity to prove to Clark that she would kill for him.

On August 3, 1980, Murray climbed into the back of his van, anticipating oral sex. Instead, Bundy shot him in the head twice and stabbed him in the back half a dozen times. When she realized the bullets in Murray's head would help the police identify her gun, she cut his head off and put it in a plastic bag, eventually dumping it in a trash can near Griffith Park.

The rest of his body was found just days later, left in his van in the parking lot at the Little Nashville club. Police began questioning regulars at the club, including Murray's wife, Jeanette. Bundy was brought down to the police station and gave detectives her version of the alibi she had already discussed with Clark, which included a detailed description of a man she had supposedly sold her two guns to.

But none of this was enough for Clark, who refused to accept any of the blame for the rapidly deteriorating situation. He told Bundy that he was moving out, and left her alone while he went out to spend time with a new girlfriend. After briefly speaking to her mother-in-law and her sons, Bundy called Geis and told him about the murders. The next morning, after being berated by Clark as she drove him to work, Bundy confessed to a co-worker about the crime spree. By the end of the day, both Clark and Bundy were arrested in relation to the series of Sunset Strip murders.

According to police commander William Booth, evidence gathered during the investigation of Murray's death, along with the information collected during the ongoing investigation into the Sunset Strip murders, let them to Clark and Bundy. Bundy would end up telling the police graphic details about each murder, admitting that she thought killing was "really fun to do."

The end of the Sunset Strip

Despite the mountains of evidence connecting Clark to the killings, he continued to claim his innocence – even after he was found guilty on six counts of murder and sentenced to death. Bundy, who had initially entered a plea of "not guilty by reason of insanity," managed to avoid a similar fate by pleading guilty to her two counts of murder. She was sentenced to two consecutive terms of 25 years to life, with an added two years for using a firearm illegally.

Until her death in 2003, Bundy fought desperately to prove Clark's innocence – even as he attempted to put all the blame on her.

CYNTHIA COFFMAN

James Marlow and Cynthia Coffman were a troubled couple who were convicted of murdering five people during a deadly rampage that spanned multiple states. The last two victims, 20-year old Corrina Novis and 19-year old Lynell Murray were kidnapped and found strangled and sodomized, and the murderous pair were found guilty of the crimes. Whereas both Marlow and Coffman received the death penalty for Novis' death, Marlow received a second death sentence for Murray's while Coffman was sentence to life without the possibility of parole in Murray's murder. Both defendants sought to shift the onus of blame to the other with Marlow claiming it was Coffman's idea to kill the girls while he only wanted to rob them and Coffman alleging that she was the victim of battered women's syndrome. Neither ploy was successful as the pair were convicted across the board for robbery, kidnapping, sodomy, and murder. Coffman has the distinction of being the first woman sentenced to death in California following the state's reinstatement of the death penalty in 1977.

Early Lives

James

James Gregory Marlow was born on 11 May 1956 in Ohio but raised in Kentucky; the son of a beautiful but amoral hillbilly woman named Doris who virtually ensured that her son would grow up completely dysfunctional. Throughout his childhood, Marlow witnessed abuse, neglect, drug use, and sex courtesy of his mother who often prostituted herself in front of him. She gave birth to another child, Veronica Koppers, in 1959 and would frequently leave her children alone or with neighbors. Marlow eventually went to live with his father, Arnold, who would beat him severely and lock him in cabinets and, subsequently, went back to his mother's house. Despite the abuse and her horrific behavior, Marlow loved his mother dearly. So much, in fact, that when he was 13 years old his mother shot him up with drugs and seduced him. During interviews Marlow openly admitted to having had sexual relations with his mother on several occasions and that he didn't know it was wrong. He loved his mother so much and thought it was normal. Experts assert that Marlow suffered from traumatic bonding in which a traumatic event—his mother's seduction—created a dysfunctional yet significant bond from which he could not escape.

By the time Marlow was 16 years old he was living alone in California and married his first of three wives. Thanks to his mother, Marlow developed a severely skewed view of women. When she died in a trailer fire he was completely distraught and "took on the sins of his parents" by turning to a life of crime and violence. In one incident when he was still a teenager, Marlow was talking to one of his cousin's girlfriend, Darlene Miller, who he—one day while driving her to a nearby convenience store—pulled over in front of an old, abandoned house and forced Miller into the house where he beat and hogtied her, and then locked her in a closet. Over a span of three days Marlow would repeatedly beat, rape, and sodomize Miller. She escaped and ran to a neighbor's house—a house that Marlow had recently burglarized. Police were called and Marlow was arrested and after a tearful pretrial interview wherein he tearfully detailed the issues with his mother, he was sent to a drug rehabilitation center in 1975 for seven months and, soon after his release in 1976 was rearrested for being under the influence. Marlow was eventually imprisoned for burglary, robbery, and drug charges and was ultimately sentenced to California's notorious Folsom Prison in 1980. It was here that Marlow—not unlike the majority of inmates—got heavily tattooed with one—a howling wolf on his right side—earning him the nickname of the Folsom Wolf.

Prior to meeting Coffman, Marlow had an extensive criminal record. On 5 November 1979 in Upland, California, Marlow and his friend Allen Smallwood, who were both heroin addicts, assaulted Jeffrey Johnson in his apartment, searched it for non-existent drugs, then took Johnson downstairs—by knifepoint—to the Liesches' apartment where they searched the second apartment for more non-existent drugs, tied up the residents—Lori and Kathy—with electrical cords, and stole some cash they had found.

The following day, Marlow entered an Upland, California, leather goods store owned by Joanne Gilligan who was helping a customer, said he had a gun in his pocket and ordered them to lie on the floor, and then robbed the register of cash and took two jackets.

At approximately 10:00 a.m. on 20 November that same year, Gertrude Smith and Wilson Lee were working at an Ontario, California, methadone clinic when Marlow and Smallwood entered brandishing a sawed-off shotgun and pistol, respectively, and demanded methadone which they were told was locked in a safe. Another employee opened the safe and the two left with methadone that had a street value of $10,000. When Marlow was finally arrested on 26 November he had a bottle of methadone in his jacket and had the shotgun wrapped in a shirt.

Cynthia

Cynthia Lynn Haskins was born on 19 January 1962 in St. Louis, Missouri. From the beginning her life was to be difficult. Born with a double hernia that precluded her mother from holding her, Cynthia never experienced the necessary mother-infant bonding so crucial for healthy adjustment. As a result, she suffered from a crucial lack of empathy and a driving propensity to seek affections elsewhere. Cynthia's father left when she was three years old and her mother—who had aspirations of becoming a singer—allegedly tried to give her and her brothers Robbie and Jeff away several times during their childhood; with Jeff eventually given up for adoption. Cynthia was frequently "farmed out" to relatives that made her become more rebellious, defiant, and reckless. By the time she was a sophomore in high school, Cynthia was already experimenting with marijuana and methamphetamine with her new friends.

Her mother remarried a successful businessman named Bill Maender with whom Cynthia did not get along. Truancy, rebelliousness, and ultimately not wanting to live by her stepfather's rules caused Cynthia to run away at age 17 to her boyfriend's, Ron Coffman, house. When Cynthia returned three months later, pregnant, abortion was not an option for her devout parents and she refused to give the baby up for adoption, so she was forced into a loveless marriage with Coffman. The marriage quickly deteriorated and Ron filed for divorce because of Cynthia's infidelities, drug use, and poor housekeeping while Cynthia accused him of physical and emotional abuse and infidelity. Cynthia then worked in a carburetor factory to take care of her son, Joshua. She ultimately abandoned Joshua after two years, leaving him with her ex-husband (allegedly intending to get him back after she got settled) although later, when she and Marlow were committing their heinous crimes she suggested that Marlow kill her ex-husband and ex-in-laws (who had legal custody of Joshua) so she could regain custody of her son. While on death row Coffman exchanges letters with her son who believes his mother to be in prison for drug-related charges. She has stated in interviews that she wants to be the one to tell him the truth someday.

There is much speculation that Coffman had antisocial personality disorder which is characterized by little regard for right and wrong or the feelings of others. Further, those with the chronic disorder tend to manipulate, antagonize, and treat others with a callous indifference, are very prone to violate the law, are easily angered, lie, behave impulsively and/or violently, and use and abuse drugs and alcohol—all without remorse or guilt. Coffman exhibited a number of these traits, many of which worsened once she began her relationship with Marlow.

In May 1984 Coffman left home with a girlfriend and journeyed west where she wound up in Page, Arizona, and moved in with her new boyfriend, Doug Huntley. The lovebirds moved to Barstow, California where Huntley had some friends. He secured employment in construction while she was a bartender and waitress and sold methamphetamines on the side. One evening they were involved in an altercation outside of a convenience store in which Coffman pulled a gun on several men who were hassling her boyfriend and this resulted in both Huntley and Coffman being arrested and jailed. While Coffman was released after a few days, Huntley became cellmates with Marlow. Huntley told Marlow all about Coffman which intrigued Marlow who, upon his release soon thereafter, showed up at Coffman's apartment. It was love at first sight as Coffman reminded Marlow of his mother and Marlow was every bit the bad boy to whom Coffman was attracted. Even after Huntley was released, Marlow, Coffman, and he remained friends until Huntley returned to prison in June of that year.

A Dangerous Partnership

Marlow and Coffman began their contentious, dysfunctional, and murderous relationship amidst drugs and violence; her former boyfriend Huntley all but forgotten. In June 1986 Marlow had Coffman drive him to Fontana, California, and to his cousin Debbie Schwab's house where he purchased methamphetamines. A few days later they went to Newberry Springs and stayed with some of Marlow's friends, Steve and Karen Schmitt. Marlow told Coffman that he was a hit man, a martial arts expert, and a White supremacist who had murdered African American while in prison. It was during this time that Coffman saw Marlow turn into "Wolf"—his angry, violent alter-ego. Coffman testified in court that Marlow would beat her and then apologize and things would be fine again for a while. This is classic cycle-of-violence behavior central to most domestic violence cases. At this point Marlow allegedly took Coffman's address book that had her mother's and son's addresses and refused to give it back to her; essentially holding it as a carrot just out of reach to get her to do what he wanted.

They traveled across the country visiting Marlow's relatives in Kentucky and Tennessee. He had told Marlow that his father had recently died and left him some land in Kentucky and that they could get her son and live as a family there. First, however, they needed a vehicle and Marlow allegedly pressured Coffman to steal her friend's red Nissan pickup truck that Marlow and friend Paul Donner painted black. Marlow and Coffman jumped in the truck, stole some license plates from an off road vehicle outside of Newberry Springs, California, and headed east.

In Woodland Park, Colorado, Marlow called Gene Kelly, a contractor who constructed microwave telephone relay towers and who Marlow had met when he was a temporary laborer for him a few years back, to see if he needed any help in Colorado at the time. (There is some discrepancy in the available literature with respect to this individual being named Gene Kelly or Elmer Lutz; however, the actual criminal case against the defendants state Kelly). Kelly told him that he didn't have any work at the time but that he would have some work in Atlanta, Georgia, in a few weeks. The couple went to Colorado Springs for a couple of days and then to St. Louis to see Coffman's grandmother. They arrived on 2 July and Coffman called her mother who was less than happy to hear from her. The couple continued their journey east.

In Pine Knot, Kentucky, Marlow called his cousin Donald "Lardo" Lyons and both he and Coffman stayed with him for several days. Marlow had expected a modest inheritance from his grandmother Lena Walls with whom Marlow and his sister Veronica were close when they were younger; however, by the time Marlow reached Kentucky there was nothing left for him. Needing money, Marlow agreed to meet with Lardo's friend Shannon "Killer" Compton and the trio discussed how a local man named Greg "Wildman" Hill was going to be testifying in court against a mutual acquaintance and that Hill should "be silenced." They arranged for Compton to give Lyons a sum of money of which Lyons would give $5,000 to Marlow to get rid of Hill.

The next day, 7 July 1986, Lyons gave Marlow a .22 caliber pistol and at 5:00 a.m. Marlow and Coffman got into their stolen black Nissan pickup and drove to Hill's house. For most of the day the two of them parked relatively close and surveilled his house, did drugs, and engaged in sex. Finally, Marlow ordered Coffman to take off her shirt and bra and to tie a bandana across her chest like a bikini top and to knock on Hill's door to elicit help for her "stalled" truck. Hill agreed and tucked his own pistol inside his jeans' waistband. At the truck, when Marlow came after Hill with his own gun, Hill drew his and after an ensuing struggle Hill's gun went off, mortally wounding him with a bullet to the head. Marlow wiped his fingerprints off Hill's gun and left it at the scene.

Lyons kept true to his word giving Marlow the $5,000 "fee" for his "hit." The next day Marlow gave the stolen Nissan to a relative and spent $3,000 on a Harley Davidson; something he wanted for a very long time. On 11 July 1986 Marlow and Coffman had a "biker" wedding atop a Marlow's new Harley. Witnesses alleged that Coffman's face was bruised and scratched from a recent beating Marlow have given her. Such violence was not an isolated incident. In fact, one time while Marlow was assaulting Coffman one of his acquaintances asked what he was doing and Marlow dislocated his arm. As a result, nobody else ever intervened when Marlow was in one of his rages against Coffman. She said that when Marlow turns into "Wolf" his voice becomes monotone and his eyes and facial expression changes—that he becomes a completely different and violent person.

Marlow ended up giving the Nissan to a friend and purchasing a 1970's Cadillac to continue their journey to Atlanta and a job with Kelly. Marlow did manage to work for four days before an incident wherein he, Coffman, and a group of coworkers went out for dinner but which turned into Marlow beating Coffman outside of the restaurant and inside the vehicle, seemingly because she assisted some men with a stuck ball at a pool table. Back at the hotel where they were staying, Marlow was not finished with Coffman. He asked her for her scissors and then queried, "Your hair or your eye?" Horrified, Coffman said her hair and Marlow cut it as short as he could with her small scissors. He then taunted her that he would pierce her eye as well before making her strip naked and forcing her to stand outside the hotel room for several minutes. He then let her back into the room where he forcibly sodomized her. The following morning Marlow found a check from Kelly that had been slid under the door for his four days of work. After a few more days of going on "pot hunts" and unsuccessfully attempting a burglary in July 1986 in Whitley County, Kentucky, the couple left and headed back to Arizona.

In Arizona, Marlow and Coffman burglarized her former boyfriend Doug Huntley's parents' house and stole their safe that contained ten silver dollars—which they kept—and some papers. They buried the safe in the dessert. The next stop was back in Newberry Springs, California, where the couple stole two rings from the Schmitts; one they pawned for cash and the other they traded for methamphetamines.

Returning to Fontana, California, in early October 1986, Marlow and Coffman stayed with his cousins, the Schwabs. During their visit Marlow tattooed "Property of Folsom Wolf" on Coffman's buttocks and the word "W-O-L-F" and some lightning bolts on her ring finger as a wedding band. They then spent some time with Marlow's friends Rita Robbeloth and her son Curtis, and then with his sister, her husband Paul Koppers, and his brother, Steve. During this time Coffman alleges that after asking for an equal share of the methamphetamine they had, Marlow became angry and beat her, threatened to kill her, forced her to consume pills he said were cyanide, extinguished a cigarette on her face, and stabbed her in the leg. The pair then went to stay with another of Marlow's friends, Richard Drinkhouse.

The Crimes

On 11 October 1986 they were linked to the death of 32-year old Sandra Neary of Costa Mesa, California who never returned from a quick trip to a local ATM machine to withdraw some money. Her car was found in a nearby parking lot and her body was later found on 24 October by some hikers near Corona, California. Their next victim was 35-year old Pamela Simmons. She was reported missing in Bullhead City, Arizona, on 28 October. Her abandoned car was found by the local police department and the theory was that she was also abducted while withdrawing money from an ATM.

Corinna Novis

On 7 November, 20-year old Corinna Novis vanished from a First Interstate Bank parking lot near a shopping mall in Redlands, California, in broad daylight. Alone, she was driving her white Honda CR-X and when she failed to make her manicure appointment at her friend Terry Davis' salon, and then failed to make a 7:00 p.m. pizza date with other friends, she was reported missing. That same day, Marlow and Coffman were at the Redlands Mall visiting his sister Koppers who worked at a restaurant and were supposed to pick her up from work; however, Marlow gave his sister back her keys, telling her that they already had a ride. Coffman, clad in a dress, and Marlow, in a suit and tie, probably seemed rather innocuous to Novis when they asked her for a ride. Earlier that day Marlow had told Coffman that they needed to "get a girl" but Coffman alleged that she did not know that Marlow intended to kill her.

At approximately 7:30 p.m., they took Novis to Marlow's friend Richard Drinkhouse's house who was home alone recovering from a motorcycle accident at the time. Coffman took their hostage into the bedroom after telling Drinkhouse they needed to use the bathroom. Marlow told Drinkhouse that Coffman was trying to get her ATM pin number so they could "rob" her bank account. Drinkhouse didn't appreciate their intrusion into his house to which Marlow assured Drinkhouse that that there wouldn't be any witnesses because how could Novis talk to anyone "if she's under a pile of rocks"? Soon thereafter, Marlow's sister Koppers showed up and she and Coffman left the house to go to a nearby 7-Eleven while Marlow cautioned Drinkhouse not to leave and then returned to the bedroom where Novis was. After Coffman returned, she went into the bedroom to change clothes and after what sounded like the shower running the three of them emerged from the bedroom—Novis' and Marlow's hair were wet (Coffman testified that she had nothing to do with "what went on in the shower"). Novis was handcuffed and had duct tape over her mouth. They left the house and Drinkhouse testified that he never saw Novis again.

The next day, Marlow and Coffman asked Drinkhouse if he wanted to buy an answering machine. Novis' employer Jean Cramer, went to check on her the morning of 10 November when she uncharacteristically failed to appear at work and didn't call. She noticed Novis' car was missing, her front door was ajar, and her bedroom was in disarray. There was no evidence of forced entry and Novis' typewriter and answering machine were missing. On 7 November Koppers sold Novis' answering machine to a friend in exchange for a half-gram of methamphetamine who sold it to someone else and the Redlands Police Department ultimately recovered it. The next day, Harold Brigham who owned the Sierra Jewelry and Loan in Fontana testified that Coffman pawned Novis' typewriter using the victim's identification.

Back at the Robbeloths' house Coffman said Marlow changed clothes and tried to access money from Novis' account at a local First Interstate Bank; however, the PIN number she gave them was incorrect. The following day they ransacked Novis' apartment, found her PIN number, stole her money, pawned the typewriter they stole, disposed of Novis' belongings and then returned to Drinkhouse's house. On 12 November Marlow found out that his sister was in police custody and he and Coffman drove to Big Bear to get rid of Novis' car. They checked into the Bavarian Lodge using a credit card from another victim, Lynell Murray. They abandoned Novis' car on a dirt road south of Santa's Village which was approximately a quarter mile off of Highway 18 in the area. Coffman's fingerprints were found on the license plate, hood, and ashtray while Marlow's prints were found on the hood. The two then proceeded to walk along Big Bear Boulevard clad only in bathing suits despite the chilly weather; the stolen clothes that they had been wearing were discarded along with the handcuffs used on Novis. Receipts for clothing purchased by Marlow and Coffman were found in the clothing's pockets. The .22 caliber pistol the couple owned was in Coffman's purse.

Novis' body was discovered on 15 November lying face down in a shallow grave at a Fontana vineyard. She had been strangled and sodomized.

Dr. Gregory Reiber performed Novis' autopsy on 17 November and conclude that time of death was between five and ten days prior. Evidence of marks on her neck, injuries to her neck muscles, and thyroid cartilage fracture suggested death by strangulation; however, the presence of dirt in her throat also suggested possible suffocation. There was also biological evidence of sodomy.

Lynell Murray

On 12 November, 19-year old psychology student and Prime Cleaners dry cleaning shop clerk Lynell Murray failed to keep a date with her boyfriend, Robert Whitecotton, in Orange County. After noticing that the cleaners looked as though it had been burglarized and ransacked and that Murray's car was parked in the parking lot out back he called the police.

Murray had no idea that the previous day Marlow and Coffman saw her leaving work and that Marlow had commented that she would be "a good one to rob." The following evening at approximately 6:00

p.m., shortly before Murray was to leave work, one Lynda Schafer entered the cleaners and dropped of some clothes with Murray. Schafer would later testify that she saw Coffman "passionately embracing a man", later identified as Marlow, in an alley behind the cleaners.

At 6:30 p.m. that evening Coffman approached Linda Whitlake who was leaving her gym and asked for a ride to her motel, claiming that her car wouldn't start. After Whitlake noticed Marlow in Novis' white car with its hood up she changed her mind about giving them a ride. Coffman said that her boyfriend had decided to call the auto club instead and Whitlake left.

At 7:13 p.m. Coffman checked into room 307 of the Huntington Beach Inn under the name Lynell Murray and used Murray's credit card. At 8:19 p.m. a Bank of America branch in Corona del Mar recorded a balance inquiry into Murray's account and a subsequent withdrawal of $80 occurred, shortly followed by a $60 withdrawal, which left a balance of $4.41. Later that evening Coffman checked into the Compri Hotel in Ontario, California, with Murray's credit card. At midnight Marlow and Coffman ate dinner at the Denny's restaurant across from the hotel, which they paid for with Murray's credit card.

Murray's body would be discovered the following day at approximately 3:00 p.m. in room 307 at the Huntington Beach Inn. Her head was in the bathtub in six inches of water with it and her face bound with strips of towel. She was gagged. Her right arm was secured to her waist with a towel. Her right leg was atop the toilet and her left leg was on the floor. Her ankles looked to have been bound with duct tape as residue was evident. Her bra, nylons, and one earring were missing and she looked to have been raped and urinated on. She had also suffered pre-mortem blunt force trauma to the head, torso injuries, two black eyes, and leg bruising which were consistent with being beaten. The cause of death was determined to be ligature strangulation.

Police finally turned their attention to Marlow and Coffman after finding Novis' driver's license and checkbook in a Taco Bell takeout bag near a dumpster in Laguna Niguel along with papers with both Marlow's and Coffman's names on them. Marlow had attempted to dispose of this damning evidence but missed the dumpster. A statewide alert was issued for both Marlow and Coffman.

Arrest

On 14 November, police were dispatched to a Big Bear, California, mountain lodge after being alerted that Murray's credit card was being used to purchase clothes at a local sporting goods store. The owner of the lodge identified Marlow and Coffman as his latest guests. After finding the lodge empty, the 100-man posse discovered the suspects walking along a mountain road at approximately 3:00 p.m. They surrendered without incident, clad in clothing they had stolen from the dry cleaning shop where Murray had worked. A few hours later Coffman led police to Novis' body. One of the victim's earrings, a .22 caliber pistol and ammunition, credit card receipts with Murray's forged signature, and a Prime Cleaners paper bag with coins were found in Coffman's purse.

The Trial

Nearly three years later Marlow and Coffman would stand trial which commenced on 18 July 1989 in San Bernardino County. At several points throughout the proceedings motions for severance filed by both defendants were denied.

Among the overwhelming evidence were both defendants' fingerprints in Novis' car and that, as previously mentioned, Coffman was linked to the Fontana pawn shop where Novis' typewriter was pawned. In room 307 of the Huntington Beach Inn where Lynell Murray's body was found, a footprint on a bathmat by her body was consistent with Marlow's boots. The aforementioned Taco Bell bag with Novis' license and checkbook and documentation with Coffman's and Marlow's names was recovered. Credit card activity demonstrated where and when the defendants had used Murray's credit card. Additionally, the discarded suit jacket that Marlow had worn when they abducted Novis was found at the Bavarian Lodge and contained identification bearing Marlow's name, various single earrings presumed to be trophies from the murders, a blue ladies wallet, and the handcuffs used on Novis. Novis' vehicle was found near Santa's Village with license plates stolen from a vehicle that was at the Huntington Beach Inn and in a nearby trash can a maintenance worker found a pillowcase containing Murray's bra and laundry receipts from the cleaners where Murray had worked.

Coffman took the stand in her own behalf, painting Marlow to be an abusive man who was violent toward her and threatened both her and her son. She alleged that any violence directed toward the victims were perpetrated by Marlow. With respect to Novis, Coffman testified that on the night of Novis' death, she had dropped Novis and Marlow off at the vineyard and was told to go purchase methamphetamines. Coffman alleges that she drove a short distance, stopped and smoked a cigarette, and then returned to "the sound of digging." Marlow returned to the vehicle alone, threw some items in the back of the car, and then started to beat her for driving away.

Coffman's attorney presented numerous witnesses who corroborated Coffman's allegations of Marlow's violence including Katherine Davis, one of Marlow's ex-wives, and her mother Marlene Boggs; Coffman's former employers in Arizona; Coffman's mother Carol Maender; and clinical psychologist Craig Rath who claimed that Coffman's relationship with Marlow was "precipitated by impaired bonding in her early life", that she was not malingering, and that she did not suffer from antisocial personality disorder.

In Marlow's defense, his sister Veronica Koppers testified about the abuse and neglect the two suffered at the hands of their mother and her father Wendell Hill; about how her father shot her mother and her mother stabbed her father seven times which prompted Doris to move to California in 1963; about visiting her mother at the Sybil Brand Institute for Women and the Frontera State Prison; about how Doris introduced her daughter to drugs much like she did with Marlow and taught her how to burglarize houses; and about the myriad drinking and drug parties hosted at their house. Several witnesses at the trial testified that Doris rarely even mentioned that she had children and paid them little attention when they were together. Despite Marlow claiming responsibility for the murder in Kentucky as well as Novis' and Murray's in California he tried to shift the majority of blame onto Coffman much as she attempted to do to him.

Throughout the trial, Coffman's legal team tried to utilize the "Patty Hearst" defense that she was brainwashed, starved, and the victim of battered women's syndrome who was subjected to frequent physical, emotional, and mental abuse. Once, she claimed, Marlow beat her with a motorcycle clutch plate bruising her face and another time kicked her with his steel-toed boots. She stated that she feared for both her life and that of her then-six-year old son. Coffman's side even presented an expert on battered women's syndrome; however, the jury apparently rejected such claims.

Other testimony suggested that Coffman was the true ringleader and cold, calculated murderess, being far more intelligent than Marlow who would do anything to keep her. At one point, prosecutor Robert Gannon asked Coffman whether her relationship with Marlow was more important than the lives of Corinna Novis and Lynell Murray to which she replied, "Yes."

Sentencing

Both defendants were convicted of the kidnapping, robbery, kidnapping for robbery, residential burglary, forcible sodomy, and murder of Novis and subsequently sentenced to death on 30 August 1989. Coffman became the first women sentenced to death in California since the state reinstated capital punishment in 1977; however, California's reputation as an overly liberal state makes it unlikely that Coffman will ever be put to death.

On 8 March 1992 Marlow received a second death sentence for Murray's murder while Coffman received a life without the possibility of parole sentence added to her death sentence, the former rather moot.

On 19 August 2004 the California Supreme Court unanimously upheld both Marlow's and Coffman's death sentences.

Post-conviction

There continues to be speculation as to whether Coffman controlled or was controlled by Marlow. In fact, while on Death Row, Marlow wrote *I Wish You Were Never Born*, a novel detailing Coffman's and his murderous spree (proceeds of the sale of his book are donated to help abused children). He asserts that their story in the popular media—including an episode of *Wicked Attractions*—was sensationalized and he wanted the truth to be known.

HUSBAND KILLER : THE TRUE STORY OF LARISSA SCHUSTER

138

ERIN EDWARDS

Larissa Leann Foreman was born January 1, 1960. She grew up on a farm near Clarence Missouri. By all accounts she had a happy childhood. She won first place at the Randolph pony show, her father, Charles, won first place in the men's division and Deeann, her mom, won second in the bareback for pleasure division. Her parents seemed to be very involved in her life. She excelled academically; she was athletic and went after what she wanted with everything she had. She was described as a 'go getter'.

Larissa graduated High school and went on to the University of Missouri Columbia to become a biochemist. She didn't come from a rich family so she would work as a nursing aide at Boone Hospital Center in Columbia Missouri. It's not known whether she liked her work as an aide, however she did like a nurse named Tim Schuster, and he liked her as well. She was electrifying and intoxicating, Tim was enthralled. They started dating after becoming friends and just hanging out together after work.

Finally, in 1982 Tim popped the question, and Larissa said yes. Between 1982 and the birth of their second child Tyler in 1990 there was a whirlwind of things happening. There was the wedding in '82, the birth of their first child, Kristin, and a move to sunny central California, Fresno to be exact.

In the beginning Tim managed the cardiology Department for St Agnes Medical Center. While Larissa worked for Pan Agricultural Laboratories. Larissa saw the company declining and thought it a good time to start her own company; Central California Research Lab. She was ambitious and worked long hours to make her company a success. Tim continued to work at St Agnes and be both Mom and Dad to their two children.

According to friends Bob and Mary Solis, Tim was the one who made sure doctor appointments were kept, homework was done and dinner was cooked and on the table. Larissa ruled her house and Tim having a non-confrontational personality went along with her, if for no other reason than to keep the peace. By this time she was making more than twice what Tim made. It was her money that made it possible for them to move to Clovis and buy a much larger home than the one they had in Fresno. It looked like they had it all...but did they?

By this time Kristen was a teenager and as with most teens there was attitude. Kristen fought with her mother at almost every turn. She stood up to Larissa in such a way that she felt she had no other option than to send her daughter to her parents in Clarence, Missouri. Tim was upset that his wife didn't even discuss this move with him; she'd decided this IS what will happen. And soon his beloved little girl was gone. But still Tim kept quiet.

The Schuster's entered into a bitter, rancorous separation in 2002, after nearly 20 years of marriage and two children. They tried living in the same house after the separation. However Larissa was not happy with this arrangement. From the very beginning she didn't want Tim to have anything to do with Tyler, no visitation and no kind of a relationship with his son at all. This was not okay with Tim. On more than one occasion she made the statement that she wished Tim would just die.

In late June or early July Larissa took Tyler and went on a trip out of state. Tim took this opportunity to secure a condo and move out of the family's home. Larissa was livid that he would have the nerve to leave while she was away and accused him of taking things from the house that didn't belong to him. What earlier seemed like idle threats became something more, she told a neighbor that she should just get it over with and kill Tim herself.

A Plan started formulating shortly after Tim moved out of the Clovis family home. Larissa asked James Fagone a lab assistant and Larissa's sometimes babysitter, sometimes whipping boy if he would help break in to Tim's house and help her get back somethings he took when he moved out. She felt he wasn't entitled to them and left messages on his answering machine telling him he'd better bring them back...or else.

After returning from a trip Tim came home to a house that had been burglarized and ransacked. One of the things missing...the very set of mixing bowls Larissa had had such a fit over. Who was her accomplice in the break-in...none other than James Fagone? Larissa wasn't shy about what they had done, she told her manicurist Terri Lopez, that after the break-in she would go back to Tim's house and sit in a chair and look around at what they had done. She also told Tami Belshay that "it gave her a feeling that was better than sex."

After the burglary the Schuster's relationship went even further downhill. Tim knew who had broken into his condo. Larissa's bitterness not only let her destroy things in the condo, but she even bragged about keying his truck. She said it made her happy every time she saw the marks on his truck. Tim seemed worried about what his estranged wife was capable of. He moved again, this time to a house in Clovis that had motion sensors and an alarm. He obtained a handgun and a permit to carry a concealed weapon. Larissa had told her manicurist Ms. Lopez that she prayed every night that Tim would just die. At one point Larissa told her that she could kill Tim and get away with it. She also asked one of the employees at CCRL if her boyfriend knew anyone that would kill Tim or at least rough him up. She'd made remarks like this before and all who heard them thought she was just venting because the divorce wasn't going the way she wanted it to. She said she would do anything to keep Tim from getting the business.

According to Bob and Mary Solis, Larissa would belittle and embarrass Tim in front friends and family alike. She seemed to relish the power she had over him.

In late June St Agnes let everyone know that there would be a round of layoffs coming and to be expecting it. Tim and his friend Mary Solis was on the short list to be let go. Larissa laughed when she heard the news. On July 9th Tim, Mary, her husband Bob and another friend Victor Uribe all had dinner together. The group broke up about 10pm that night, before Tim left the Solis' they had made arrangements to meet for breakfast the next morning. Tim never showed for his exit meeting or for breakfast. This worried Bob and Mary, it seems Tim was never late for anything, and if he thought he was going to be late he called. He was also supposed to pick up Tyler that evening.

His friends tried to reach Tim, calling his cell phone. Finally they called Uribe and told him that they couldn't reach Tim and would he go by the house and check on their friend. Uribe arrived at Tim's house and went inside. There didn't seem to be anything out of place, until he went to the bedroom. Tim's watch, wallet and cell phone were lying on the dresser. Uribe was now worried as well. Victor said "He never went anywhere without his cell, he kept it with him at all times, in case the kids needed him."

No one knew what had happened to Tim. The police refused to even take a missing person's report until he'd been missing 24 hours. July 10th when Tim had not been heard from in the allotted time Bob Solis filed the missing person's report. Officer John Willow from the Clovis Police Department responded to the call.

Willow found Tim's handgun under a cushion of a chair. He found Tim's cell phone in the bedroom and called all the numbers in his contacts to see if any of them had seen or heard from Mr. Schuster. When he called Larissa she said she hadn't heard from him either. He also talked to Terri Lopez and she relayed to Willow that the Schuster's were going through a rather nasty divorce. John Willow decided to turn the case over to Detectives Larry Kirkhart and Vincent Weibert.

When they entered Tim's home they noted some damage on the wall behind the chair where the gun was found earlier. They found a briefcase in the same room as the chair. Inside they found a microcassette recorder and tape. In the bedroom they found an answering machine that showed only one number, a cell phone number belonging to Larissa Schuster. Detective Kirkhart then asked Larissa to come to the police station for a chat about her missing husband.

During her interview with the detectives she told them that she and Tim were getting a divorce and that they did not communicate very well with each other. They asked her about her cell number being on the caller ID. She fabricated a story about being asleep on her couch and waking up to find she had pushed some buttons and maybe she had speed dialed Tim. They asked her if she had her phone with her and she said no. Kirkhart called for a pause in the interview and went to the parking lot to find Larissa's car. He looked in the window and saw a phone on the center console, dialed her number and the phone in the car rang.

Kirkhart went back to the interview room and asked Larissa to come with them to unlock her car and retrieve her phone. Back inside the station the interview resumed. The detective went through her contacts that she had on speed dial, none of them were Tim's number.

Larissa's whole demeanor changed, she was shaking and in the opinion of the detectives showing signs of deceit. She came clean and admitted that she had lied to the detectives and she knew she shouldn't have. She claimed she wasn't trying to be deceitful. None the less they let Schuster go home, for now. At this point in their investigation they still had no idea what had happened to Tim. Kirkhart had asked Larissa if she thought that Tim could just cash out some money and leave town, go camping or to Vegas to just get away. She told them she didn't think he would do that, that he wouldn't leave his son like that. This was still just a missing person case and most of Tim's friends thought that perhaps he had just had enough, the divorce, the custody battle, losing his job was to much for him to handle. Tami Belshay, Bob and Mary Solis and Victor Uribe were among those friends. The detectives were thinking the same thing at this point.

With no solid leads on Tim's whereabouts detectives Weibert and Kirkhart kept searching for some clue, however small that might give them some direction on finding Tim. Kirkhart was going through Tim's ledger provided to them by Larissa. And they came across a name they were familiar with…James Fagone. They knew his name because he was the one suspected of breaking into Tim's house with Larissa shortly after Tim moved out of the family home a year earlier. They also knew that he was an associate of sorts of Larissa's.

The following Monday Detectives Kirkhart and Daly called Fagone to come and talk with them. Vince Weibert thought that perhaps Fagone might have some "inside" information on Tim's disappearance.

It seems that Fagone was a babysitter for the Schuster's son Tyler, before and after their separation. James was a good kid according to his attorney Peter Jones. "He's an above average student, higher than a 4.0 grade point average…a gentle spirit."

Fagone was nervous during the police interview. He admitted that Larissa had him help her break into Tim's house and take back things that she didn't want him to have.

James told the detectives that Larissa was going around the house looking for things and he just wanted to get the TV and some other stuff so he wasn't paying attention to what she was doing. Obviously James was scared out of his mind by now, but they pressed him more telling him they "knew he was involved somehow" with Tim's disappearance. Fagone's determination not to tell what had happened, what him and Larissa Schuster had done crumbled.

Fagone confessed that he had been there the night that Tim went missing, that he had gone to his house with a weapon. James relayed to them that Larissa had paid him the $2000 to purchase a stun gun and that he could just keep the rest for himself.

So as the day wore on James conveyed the sordid details of the night in questions.

On the night that Tim lost his job at St Agnes and had dinner with a group of friends, James had done what he was told to do by

Larissa, buy a stun gun. Later he would get the call from her (Larissa). She picked him up and went to Tim's house. James laid in wait in the darkness just outside of his door. He could hear Larissa on the phone telling Tim that Tyler wasn't feeling well and she needed him to come to the front door.

A few moments later Tim opened the front door and James sprung from the shadows and attacked him wrestling him to the ground. Tim was struggling; James was using the stun gun on him, on the arm at first, not sure where else he might have zapped him. Soon Tim stopped struggling and when James looked up he saw Larissa with a rag that had been soaked in chloroform.

Were the detectives hearing this right? Was Fagone confessing to the murder of Timothy Schuster? But if they were going to believe any of it they needed some kind of evidence. They asked about the stun gun again, and what had Fagone done with it. He told them he threw it in a portable toilet on the edge of town. The investigators found the stun gun, right where James told them it should be.

Now at the same time Fagone was being interviewed Clovis Police Department got a call from a woman saying that her boss ask her to do something that in retrospect seemed a little off, suspicious even. Her Boss...Larissa Schuster. Leslie Dodd had been instructed to rent a moving truck by her boss. She was told to use her personal credit card and rent it in her own name not her boss's. A year earlier Larissa had asked the same employee to rent a storage unit near Schuster's lab, again to do it in the employees name and with her personal credit card.

Jim Koch got the call to check it out. He went to the storage unit and walked down the hall. He had been told to look for a blue barrel. When he found Schuster's unit and opened the door "there was a very very strong odor." Koch said. "I had on a breathing apparatus and gloves."

He saw the blue barrel, he opened it.

Koch said in an interview, "And when I opened the barrel I—I saw something that was very, very shocking to me and I recognized immediately as human remains. There was a barrel that's over 3/4 of the way full of fluid and portions of—of—body protruding from the fluid. And the body was obviously decaying. It was placed in acid. And the acid was basically eating away at the body."

Had Larissa Schuster killed her husband and put him in the barrel? According to James Fagone, yes she had, and he had helped her and then watched as she poured a caustic solution in on top of Tim. Worst of all, Tim was probably still alive when the acid was poured on him and he was sealed inside the barrel.

Tim had been found, the truth had come out and the Clovis detectives were on their way to Missouri to arrest Larissa for the murder of her husband Tim. They met her at the airport where she had gone to see her family. According to the detectives that arrested her for the murder she didn't even ask what had happened to Tim or how he died.

Both James Fagone and Larissa Schuster were arrested and charged with 1st degree murder.

Now that the perpetrators of Tim Schuster's murder had been arrested it was time to take them to trial. The murder was committed in the early morning hours of July 10, 2003. There was a lot left to do before the trial could begin.

The Clovis police department had to finish gathering evidence, talk to friends and family to make sure that everything was done correctly. They wanted to make sure that Larissa and James would not be let go on a technicality.

The judge had to decide if he would make this a death penalty case or a life in prison without parole case. That would be decided later. The prosecutor had to prepare a rock solid case and present the evidence to a jury in a manner that would guarantee a conviction. The defense would also be talking to people on behalf of their clients. Find people that had nothing but good things to say about them in hopes of offsetting the horrible truths that would come out at trial.

The judge separated the cases and James and Larissa would be tried separately. James was tried first. His attorney portrayed James as a misguided man who hero worshipped Larissa.

He was found guilty and is now serving a life without parole sentence.

There was so much media coverage on Larissa that the defense asked and received a change of venue. Her trial was moved to Los Angeles.

Monday October 22, 2007 Larissa's trial started. Prosecutor Dennis Peterson relayed to the jury of 9 women and 3 men just how the murder went down. He told them that Tim was still alive when the acid was poured over him while he laid head first inside the blue barrel. Her motive? She didn't want to share anything that they built during their 19 ½ years of marriage. She felt Tim didn't deserve any part of the business, or home and didn't want him to have contact with their tween son, Tyler.

CCRL employees would also testify to the facts of the blue barrel being at the lab and the day Tim was reported missing went to look for it and it was gone. They also said that Larissa had said that she should just shove Tim in the barrel and get rid of him.

A large amount of Hydrochloric acid, 12 gallons and Sulfuric acid, 4 gallons was ordered for Schuster's lab, more than ever before. Leslie Dodd (nee Fichera) testified that, "that was more acid than the lab would use in a year."

Joseph Boatwright thought Larissa was joking when she asked "if he thought a body would fit in the blue barrel."

Juror's watched several hours of Larissa's police interview. She made Tim out to be controlling and having a volatile temper. After seeing that part of the interview Bob Solis testified to the contrary, that Tim was very calm and a non-violent, non-confrontational person.

In another part of the interview with Clovis Detectives Schuster stated that "she prayed that Tim would get over this hostility about the divorce." Her manicurist Terri Lopez told a different story. Lopez said that "she told me she prayed every night he would die."

A hair stylist Becky Holland sometimes did Larissa's hair. During those appointments Larissa would rant about Tim. Holland didn't think much about it because she knew they were going through a divorce. Later though she said the hateful remarks escalated, Holland told the court, "this is getting a little creepy. It was so intense."

The jurors got to hear just how intense it was when they got to hear message after message of Larissa calling her husband awful names and making threats about their children. The prosecutor used these recordings to make a point to the jury; Larissa was in a "murderous rage". Nuttall interjected that these messages were left on Tim's machine 7 months before the murder.

And with this the prosecution rested, hoping that they had proved their case. There was one witness that they really needed to be able to lockdown the case against Schuster, they needed James Fagone. The judge had barred his confession so the jury would never hear in his own words what happened July 10, 2003. But he refused to cooperate with Peterson because he had already filed his appeal. The only thing that might have helped Peterson is the fact that James Fagone had already been convicted of Tim's murder.

Nuttall began the defense's case by telling the jury that neither he nor his client could tell them what had happened to Tim because "we don't know". And since the jury heard nearly nothing about Fagone, Roger Nuttall blamed the murder on him. After all Fagone had already been found guilty of the murder Larissa was now on trial for. Nuttall said in his opening statements that "Tim was an angry man who belittled Larissa in over-compensation for his own failings as a husband and father." And that "he began stalking Larissa after the divorce proceedings started."

Now Defense attorney Nuttall brought in a stream of witnesses that would steer the blame away from his client.

He had a medical expert that said the victim's body was cut in half and that the police had completely missed a second crime scene and the evidence from there would have proved that Fagone and others were responsible for Tim's murder not Larissa.

Nuttall even had psychiatrist Stephen Estner on the stand. Estner said that, "My impression was that Mrs. Schuster was a very direct and assertive person, and Mr. Schuster was a more passive and nurturing personality. And I think they started butting heads over that."

Larissa Schuster took the stand in her own defense and adamantly denied the charges saying, "No, I did not kill my husband." Again James Fagone would have the whole murder put squarely on him. Schuster told the jury, ""I heard him say something like 'there had been an accident and Tim is dead.' I thought he was joking."

She said that the $2000 payment to Fagone was for babysitting Tyler and housesitting while she was away on vacation with her son. Schuster said the large amount of acid was for cleaning a large scale of lab glass. Schuster seemed to explain everything away poking holes in the prosecutor's case. Would it be enough to get an acquittal? Had she actually swayed the jury?

It seemed that the trial was plagued with problems, including accusations of juror misconduct. At least one juror was replaced by an alternate due to disruptive behavior. Another admonished for giving Larissa a 'thumbs up' after her testimony. And yet with all of that...it was time for the jury to deliberate of the weeks of testimony they'd heard.

It took a little more than two days for the jury to decide on a verdict.

Guilty of Murder with a special circumstance of financial gain. The verdict came exactly one year after Fagone's.

Roger Nuttall slowed the sentencing of Larissa Schuster while he tried to find reasons to ask for a new trial. He even used the argument that there may have been juror misconduct. Nuttall wanted to talk to the jurors but Ellison said no. Nuttall appealed and the District court of Appeals told Ellison to contact the jurors on Schuster's behalf. All the jurors and alternates refused to speak to her attorney.

So on May 8, 2008, five months after being found guilty of her estranged husband's murder Larissa Leeann Schuster was sentenced to life in prison without the possibility of parole. Judge Ellison also denied her request for a new trial.

At the sentencing a total of seven people stood up to make statements about how they had been affected by the murder of Timothy Allen Schuster.

Kristen, Tim and Larissa's oldest child and only daughter made an emotionally charged statement to and about her mother.

She called her mother a demon for "taking my father away." And told her. "I pray you're continually haunted at night by the sight and sound of my father fighting for his last breathing moments on this earth. I hope you toss and turn and have horrible nightmares visualizing the horrific act of violence you have committed. Maybe later in life I can learn to forgive you, but I doubt it. This is goodbye, not just for now, but forever. This is goodbye as your daughter."

Kristen was so devastated over her father's murder she reached out to a support group murdervictims.com. Several people shared their own experiences of losing a parent at a young age hoping she could find at least a little peace.

ALICIA SHAYNE LOVERA

The life of Alicia Shayne Lovera looked like something out of a soap opera.

Born into poverty, she was ushered into a life of wealth and privilege when her mother married a rich president of a bank. She grew up to be beautiful, popular and spoiled. But she soon find herself in financial ruin when her stepfather committed suicide, leaving the family with nothing.

Her sense of entitlement still intact, she married a struggling math teacher who couldn't resist her charms.

But when the marriage became an inconvenience, she did what all black widows do.

She killed her husband.

This is her story.

EARLY LIFE

Alicia Shayne Good was born in 1966 to teenage parents. Going by her middle name Shayne, her early life wasn't easy as her parents lacked the necessary resources to provide. Her mother would divorce her father. But when Shayne turned seven-years old things to a turn for the better.

"Her mother and she were poor," journalist Jamie Satterfield said. "Her mother met Brent Mills who was a bank president and they married into that family and Brent adopted Shayne."

The change in life circumstance was jarring to the young Shayne. She was instantly given an upgrade in lifestyle as she the world was now her oyster. There were expensive vacations, cars and garish parties.

Her new stepfather, Brent Mills, was a bank executive who treated Alicia and her mother Sandy to all the spoils his job could bring. He was well regarded in the business community and had several contacts.

But Brent had inherited the bank built by his father and lacked his business acumen. He was lenient in granting loans and the bank soon grew insolvent. He was also suspected of using the bank as a money laundering service for drug dealers.

On the surface, Brent told the family that the allegations were all fraudulent. He gave them every assurance that everything would be okay.

Then he killed himself.

"He took a gun to his head and blew his brains out," forensic psychologist Paula Orange said. "That left an indelible image on Shayne's outlook on life."

His suicide would leave the family in financial ruin. The papers would ridicule Mills, giving voice to all of the wild allegations of his mismanagement. The family would be left shamed and with nothing.

The effect was devastating on Shayne. She would go from being the richest girl in the school to being dirt poor.

Again.

Shayne just wanted to get away. She had entertained aspirations of being broadcast anchor, thinking that her beauty and speaking skills would lead to an easy gig. So she decided to move out of state for college. She would attend a university in Missouri where she would meet Kelly Lovera.

They would marry a year later.

The couple would have two children over the next five years despite being the polar opposites temperamentally.

Kelly was cool, calm and wanted a quiet life. He didn't embrace the partying lifestyle that Shayne wanted.

"Theirs was a union that is hard to comprehend," Orange said. "Kelly was not en route to becoming the next bank president. He was a twenty-year old student who was struggling. He wanted to be a math teacher. Shayne wanted to live a hedonistic lifestyle. She wanted to party and spend lavishly. Why they would get married defies explanation."

Bored in Missouri, Shayne would then convince Kelly to move back to her hometown in Tennessee. Kelly would consent to the move.

A RETURN TO POVERTY

The couple would live in Sevierville which was thirteen miles north of her former luxury home in Gatlinburg. But it was light years away in terms of affluence as they were forced to rent out a small, one story townhouse.

The neighborhood they lived in was called "Frog Alley".

"A luxury once experienced becomes a necessity," Orange said. "Shayne had gotten used to living the high life. But married life, particularly one with of a lack of resources, would prove to be difficult for her."

"Frog Alley was a place for the working poor," Satterfield said. "To come back and live there would be extremely embarrassing for her."

Kelly's focus was not on making money. He was working on his master's degree in mathematics while he took a teaching position at Pellissippi College in Knoxville. Shayne would work various odd jobs to help the family make ends meet and was not happy about that.

"She had wild ambitions to become a news anchor," Orange said. "But she didn't do anything to make that happen. She wanted someone else to do all the work for her just like she experienced when her step-father financed her life."

BOREDOM SETS IN

Shayne entertained neighbors for barbecues and poker nights. The problem is, the only people that seemed to come around were other men.

She was thoroughly bored with her marriage and began to have multiple affairs.

"She would flirt with men in full view of the children," Orange said. "Men would come over ostensibly to play cards. She would play 'footsie' with them underneath the poker table. She didn't want to be a mother and got bored with that act. She wanted to party, to be the rich wild girl that she was as a teenager. The idea of staying home with a boring math teacher and two needy children was anathema to her. She wanted a way out."

The affairs would occur in her apartment when Kelly was away. Different men would come and go at various hours.

"He's (Kelly) cramping my style," Shayne told one of her lovers. "And you're so much better than him."

"Thanks," her lover said with a grin.

"Do you know anything about how to poison someone?"

"Excuse me?"

"You know," Shayne said. "How certain poisons are undetectable."

Shayne would test the waters with her lovers. She would ask them about poisons in a joking manner. But then they would soon realize that she was serious. There was an ulterior motive to her affairs.

She wanted to find someone to kill her husband.

And she would find a willing assassin in Brett Rae.

THE NEXT DOOR NEIGHBOR

Brett was young and inexperienced with women. He had never encountered anyone like the sexy Shayne Lovera.

"Brett fell very hard for Shayne," Satterfield said. "Their affair started very quickly. And it was hot and heavy."

"Brett was a rich kid," Satterfield said. "His father was a newspaper publisher (Rick Rae, a Canadian publisher of the Sevier County newspaper). He was a well-to-do guy. He was just wild. He was just one of those people who was 'full-on' all of the time. He was up for anything."

And he was completely infatuated with Shayne.

Shayne set up Brett the same way she set up her other lovers. After a torrid session of lovemaking, she popped the question.

Will you kill my husband?

"I'll do anything for you," he told her with baited breath.

Shayne offered him a deal.

"If he were to get rid of Kelly," Satterfield said. "Then he would get her. That's what Brett wanted."

"Brett let his little head do the thinking for his big head," Orange said. "He was going to inherit money from his father so he had absolutely nothing to gain by killing Shayne's husband. Nothing except sex which of course if he had money, he would have more options than a narcissistic married woman. He simply did not have the life experience to see Shayne for what she was."

She would have a party on November 5th, 1994, an outdoor barbecue with gambling and drinking. Kelly left the party early and went to sleep on the couch.

Brett would be the last one to leave that evening. On his way out the door, they both noticed Kelly asleep on the couch.

"It was a spontaneous thing," Orange said. "They didn't have a murder weapon so they used whatever was immediately available. That would be the baseball bat of Kelly's son."

Kelly would then be bludgeoned to death.

"The plan was to put him in his own vehicle," Satterfield said. "And make it look like an accident."

Brett then dragged Kelly into his jeep and drove down Highway 14. He parked near an embankment and pushed the jeep down the side, watching it carom into a tree.

He then called one of his friends to pick him up.

Brett did not keep the news of the murder to himself. He would brag to two of his friends of what he had done.

"I put him (Kelly) over a hundred foot embankment," Brett said. "I fucked his wife and killed his ass. She told me I'd get more sex and more money if I get rid of him so I did."

Brett told his friends of the other methods he thought of using to kill Kelly but that he decided to beat him to death with the baseball bat then "stage a car crash."

FINDING THE BODY

A pair of tourists would discover Kelly's black jeep below the road. Inside, they would see his bloodied dead body. Initially, they believed that he was the victim of an accident. They called the authorities and reported that it appeared as if his jeep had gone off the road and hit a tree

Park Ranger Jerry Grubb was notified of the "accident" at the Great Smoky Mountains National Park.

The whole scene, however, looked suspicious from the get-go.

"Just wasn't any skid marks," Grubb said. "No disturbed gravel. There just wasn't any disturbance in that area."

Grubb looked inside the jeep and found the body of Kelly Lovera, laying in a pool of blood trailing toward the front seat. The blood should have been trailing behind the victim if he had, in fact, struck the tree head on.

Additionally, Kelly's injuries were not consistent with a car crash victim. The facial injuries appeared to be the result of a beating, not the impact of the jeep against the tree.

MURDER ON THEIR HANDS

The autopsy would reveal that Kelly had been beaten to death and a homicide investigation ensued. Authorities would then visit Shayne's apartment and inform her of her husband's death.

She would go into hysterics, sobbing uncontrollably.

"Do you know why anyone would want to do this to him?" an investigator asked.

"He doesn't have any enemies!" she bawled.

But an officer would notice blood splatter on the glass of Kelly's diploma that was placed on a wall near the couch. They would obtain a search warrant and a crime team would arrive, spraying luminol over the apartment.

Luminol lightens up blood stains when a fluorescent ray is scanned over it.

"The whole living room lit up like a Christmas tree," Orange said. "That is when they knew they had the guilty party."

Detectives then began to question neighbors who all pointed their fingers at Brett Rae, the lover of Shayne.

Both Shayne and Brett were arrested and charged with first-degree premeditated murder.

Brett would confess quickly. He admitted to using the baseball bat and then staging the car wreck. He would be represented by Robert Ritchie who would prep him for the murder trial for nearly three months. Ritchie, however, would notice that Brett was completely obsessed with Shayne. He then turned the case over to Robert Ogle but two weeks before the trial Alan Feltes was brought in as Brett was given joint representation.

"His attorneys were flabbergasted at his refusal to give up Shayne," Orange said. "He was truly in love with her and wanted to protect her even if it meant incriminating himself."

"I did it," Brett insisted. "Just leave her out of it."

Feltes told Brett that there was no way he could win the case with all of the evidence stacked against him. The only thing Brett cared about was putting Shayne in jeopardy.

THE TRIAL

Park Ranger Jerry Grubb would testify against the killing duo, presenting the forensic evidence found at the home and jeep. Friends and family would testify that both Shayne and Brett had bragged to them about what they had done.

Going in desperation mode, Shayne would then take the stand. She wanted to tell her version of what happened that night.

"Brett had stopped by to talk to me when Kelly came out and confronted him," Shayne said. "They began fighting and Brett picked up a baseball bat. He swung it only to keep Kelly away. But then he accidentally hit him and killed him."

Shayne would go on to say that she didn't witness any of this. She was asleep and really knew nothing that happened.

"Brett and I were not lovers," Shayne said. "We were nothing more than neighbors. It was a case of fatal attraction. He had a thing for me and wanted to kill my husband."

She didn't know, however, that when both she and Brett were released on bail they were followed by a Siever County Sheriff. He followed them into the mountains and saw them having intercourse in the woods.

When Shayne was confronted with this evidence, she tried to regroup.

"I had sex with Brett," Shayne said. "But only because I had to. He threatened to involve me in the murder plot. My purpose in going there was trying to save what little bit of life I had left at that point."

The explanation did not go over well with the jury. It took them only an hour and a half to return with a guilty verdict.

OFF TO JAIL

On January 29th, 1996, both Shayne and Brett would be convicted of Kelly's murder. They would not be given the death penalty, however. The prosecution wanted a sentence of life without parole.

Feltes approached by the attorneys for Shayne. They stated that a plea agreement would be possible but it would have to be a package deal with Brett.

Feltes advised Brett to take the deal as the plea agreement would guarantee him a life sentence with possibility of parole. If he didn't take the deal, the odds would be that he would be facing life without parole.

"Just don't do anything to hurt Shayne," Brett said. "I want to see her."

"What?"

"I want to see her before I take the deal."

Brett would persist in wanting to see Shayne. Instead he would take the deal.

"His attorneys described him as having the saddest eyes they had ever seen in a courtroom," Orange said. "He was truly in love with Shayne. She, on the other hand, threw him under the bus. She was willing to say whatever it took to get herself off and it backfired."

THE AFTERMATH

Kelly's children would be placed into the care of his parents. Brett and Shayne would receive life with parole after twenty-five years.

Brett would later try to appeal his sentencing despite agreeing to a plea bargain which barred him from doing so.

His claim would be rejected.

Ray would write that "his trial was ineffective for encouraging him to accept the state's offer of life with possibility of parole; failing to prepare for mitigating circumstances at the sentencing phase; failing to properly conduct a pre-trial investigation; failing to adequately consult with him during critical stages of the proceedings; failing to advise him of his rights to direct appeal and collateral attack of his conviction; deficient performance of counsel at trial; his guilty plea was coerced and involuntary; and his conviction is void as violating the protection against double jeopardy."

"He had conceded his guilt during the guilty plea hearing and that his attorneys did the best they could...he made these admissions only because the attorneys instructed him to do so and although he agreed that he believed himself to be guilty of first degree murder at the time of his plea, he now retracts that admission."

Brett's attorney Feltes would dispute his allegations, stating that he "never had any problem with Brett being incoherent or not understanding anything he was told or advised."

Both Brett and Shayne remain in prison, waiting to be paroled in 2025.